pink houses
and **family** taverns

with a foreword by
michael martone

photographs by
raymond bial and katharine wright

pink houses
and family taverns

becky bradway

INDIANA
University Press

Bloomington & Indianapolis

The publisher thanks Millikin University for their assistance in the production of this book.

This book is a publication of

Indiana University Press
601 North Morton Street
Bloomington, Indiana 47404-3797 USA

http://iupress.indiana.edu

Telephone orders 800-842-6796
Fax orders 812-855-7931
Orders by email iuporder@indiana.edu

The paper used in this publication meets the minimum requirements of American National Standard for Information Sciences—Permanence of Paper for Printed Library Materials, ANSI Z39.48-1984.

Manufactured in the United States of America

Library of Congress Cataloging-in-Publication Data

Bradway, Becky, date
 Pink houses and family taverns / Becky Bradway ; with a foreword by Michael Martone ; photographs by Raymond Bial and Katharine Wright.
  p. cm.
  ISBN 0-253-34088-8 (alk. paper) — ISBN 0-253-21522-6 (pbk. : alk. paper)
  1. Decatur Region (Ill.)—Social life and customs—20th century. 2. Decatur Region (Ill.)—Rural conditions. 3. Country life—Illinois—Decatur Region. 4. Bradway, Becky, date 5. Decatur Region (Ill.)—Biography. I. Title.
  F549.D3 B73 2002
  977.3'582—dc21
                                    2001005439

1 2 3 4 5 07 06 05 04 03 02

to paige and doug
who put up with my divided attention
with so much good humor

Believe it or not, you won't find that place so hot
If you ain't got the Do-Re-Mi. . . .

—WOODY GUTHRIE

Daddy won't you take me back to Muhlenberg County
Down by the Green River where paradise lay
I'm sorry my son but you're too late in asking
Mister Peabody's coal train has hauled it away.
. . .
When I die let my ashes float down the Green River
Let my soul roll on up to the Rochester dam
I'll be halfway to Heaven with Paradise waitin'
Just five miles away from wherever I am.

—JOHN PRINE

If you know your history
Then you would know where you're coming from
Then you would not have to ask me
Who the hell I think I am

—BOB MARLEY

It's not like life's such a veil of tears
It's just full of thoughts that act as souvenirs
for those tiny blunders made in yesteryears
that compromise Jacob Marley's chain.

Well, I had a little metaphor to state my case
it encompassed the condition of the human race
but to my dismay, it left without a trace
except for the sound of Jacob Marley's chain.

—AIMEE MANN

CONTENTS

getting out to other places

contents

xii

foreword: passing through normal

I live now next to the Country Club in Tuscaloosa, Alabama. I overlook the ninth green, a par three, and frequently find golf balls in my front yard. The front yard came with a cement life-sized authentically painted deer. The concrete is sloughing off in spots, exposing a tendon of rebar on a back leg and antennae of rusty wire rooted in the antlers. I have spent the four years I've lived here digging up the fairway grass of my big front lawn to plant clumps of decorative grass. Those clumps need cutting just once a year instead of twice a week and produce, in the fall, flower plumes and foxtails that smoke and float all through the mild winter.

This neighborhood was built after the Second World War. I like to imagine its conception as a dream in the trenches and hedgerows of that war, a soldier's vision, someone's ideal of home and heaven, as far as you can get from the field of battle. But the money in this town has all gone north of the Black Warrior River where bigger newer houses ring bigger greener courses, leaving my little neck of the woods looking a bit worse from wear, a kind of shabby elegance. That is how I could afford to buy a house here, the slow decline.

Recently, my parents drove from Indiana to visit. They parked the car in the driveway. Not long after they arrived, there was a knock at the front door. A man there identified himself as Lee, a neighbor from down around the sixth tee who happened to see the Indiana plates on my parents' car.

"You're from Fort Wayne, I bet," he said. The numbers on the tags are coded to the counties of the state. It turned out that Lee had just moved back to Alabama after living in Fort Wayne for forty years, working in a factory there. We stood in the front room talking about the people we knew in common, the places and stores, the restaurants and high school teams. I had moved south to take a job. Lee's family forty years ago had headed north for the same reason. "I came back home," he said.

It happened twice more during my parents' visit, people stopping us to say they, too, were from Indiana or had been from the state, since now they had come back home to Alabama after living up north for most of their lives.

It is happening again, you know, another leg of this endless migration. Fifty, sixty, one hundred years ago the countryside and even whole little towns in Alabama, Mississippi, the South emptied out, the inhabitants streaming north following other visions, tracking dreams up the Illinois Central, the GM&O, the Southern. The passenger trains are gone but the current models of the cars these migrants built for all those years up north will serve as transportation.

America is described as a nation of immigrants but has never produced its own emigrants. Its migrations are all internal. And they are pretty much invisible. The great flux and hubbub of the 20th century, the tectonic shift of the rural to the urban happened, as Wendell Berry points out, one farm at a time. This seems to me to be the great drama of America: the necessity and the ability to move pitched against the desire and the need to stay. The longing to belong or the itch to get gone.

Pink Houses and Family Taverns is about a lot of things in particular but on the whole it is about this drama. In the essays, Becky Bradway writes compellingly about the place where she was raised and still lives, but she also knows that the hidden component of place is time and its ceaseless motion and the motion it spawns in all of us. On these many stable planes, we are always passing through.

There is a lot of driving in these pages. There are also whole essays on porches. There is much contemplation of "the road" while the author hunches over her very stationary desk. Here, even the houses have wheels but those houses haven't moved in decades. That doesn't mean that in the next moment they won't. Here, the landscape of Illinois, so vast and flat, appears so fixed, so permanent. Yet how much better is this horizontal topography for everything and everyone to slide, skim, and skate over its surface. These are essays about moving and not moving, the vibration of molecules in the matrix of sheet steel. Nothing finally stays put in this place that seems so in place.

Becky Bradway, in piece after piece, captures the forces of this compression and suspension, this isometric pressure, this shimmering tension in the surface of a soap bubble the moment before it bursts. These essays are exercises in active stillness, which seems particularly Midwestern, a regional response to being swept over by the frontier, blown by by migration after migration, even sanded down to dust by wave after wave of glacier. It is, she suggests, where life has felt temporary for a very long time.

I am reading these essays miles away from my home. I am writing this essay in my home in Alabama. Here I am digging up grass to plant grass. I am waiting for a knock at the door, a visit from a stranger who knows me. I live in someone else's dream home dreaming of my home in Indiana. I haven't stayed put. But Indiana and its neighborhood haven't either.

MICHAEL MARTONE
Tuscaloosa

acknowledgments

Earlier versions of these essays have appeared in the following publications: "The Better Porch," *Creative Nonfiction;* "Defending the Land," *The North American Review;* "Pink Houses and Family Taverns," *Troika;* "Dancing Lines and Squares" and "Blading B/N," *Another Chicago Magazine;* "Ask Lord Byron," *Brilliant Corners: A Journal of Jazz and Literature;* "The Language of Grace," *South Carolina Review;* "Confirmation," *Third Coast.*

Since this is my first published book, I have a life's worth of people to thank. But this would be long and boring (except, maybe, to the people being thanked), so I'll try to keep it to those who helped the most in the writing and publishing of these essays.

My editor, Kendra Boileau Stokes, from Indiana University Press, took an interest in this book and directed its production from the time it hit her desk to the time it was printed. You probably wouldn't have this book in your hands if it hadn't been for Kendra. I also want to thank my agent, Irene Moore, who always reminds me of audience and of getting the work out. And Michael Martone, a generous reader, who found the time.

As for teachers, I'm grateful to Curtis White, who never condescended, Charlie Harris, whose feedback on my dissertation taught me accountability, and John Knoepfle, for being a professional writer at just the right time for me.

Those friends who most influenced my writing are from my old Springfield group. They weren't with me when I wrote this book, through no fault of theirs, but they were the ones who remained in my mind as my listeners. In no particular order:

Martha Miller, Myra Epping, Gary Smith, Keith Kelley, Townsend Regahr, Tim Osburn, Gael Carnes, Herb Beuoy, George Painter, Ross Hulvey, Peg Knoepfle, Jane Morrel, Corlyss Disbrow, Tavia Ervin, and everyone else who passed through in those wild Springfield days. I miss you guys! And thanks to Kim Dozier and Kirsti Sandy, fellow former students at ISU, for your questions.

Millikin University people: What would I do without the rowdy creative writing students who remind me to stay irreverent; the music and theater students who remind me to be innocent in art; and the serious, politically minded students who remind me to be not *too* irreverent? I'm glad to have energetic and cheerful colleagues who toss around ideas when they're not being frantic—particularly Dan Guillory when he talks writing. Finally, I'm grateful to work with Jim Perley, Dean of Arts and Sciences, whose office contributed funding for the photography in this book.

Photographers: Thanks to Ray Bial for his kind portrayal of small town folks and to Katharine Wright for producing her delicate works. You put in considerable time to make this a pretty book.

I would also like to thank my family for giving me so many great stories. My late mom, Connie Bradway, stood by me as I tried to figure it all out. My cousins Mike, Brenda, Joe, and Kirk were with me over those long and free river days—they keep me grounded. And, of course, thanks to my husband, Doug, and my kids Paige, Andrew, and Monica, who learned to live with having an arty type in the family.

If I left you out, I'll buy you a beer. If I put you in, you can buy *me* a beer.

photographs

photographs

here
and now in
soy city

OVERCOME

THE COMMUNITY was against the school board's decision until Jesse Jackson came to town. Then Decatur, Illinois, got posted  over the news like some slapped-up wanted poster and the city drew its lines.

"We were on CNN."

"They showed the video-tape of the game. I've seen fights like that a million times."

"Looked to me like those kids were beating the crap out of that guy," said Evan, who had gone to that same high school.

"Can we go to the march? Come on, it's learning. We'll write something about it." After all, they said, this is a writing class and we're writing about place, and the demonstration is in a place, so. . . ."

"If we go outside, I can smoke," J.J. cracked to her friends.

"Please let us go! It's history!"

When a place grabs the world's attention, it's because of trouble. We hear the name years later, only to recall an unpleasant familiarity, a recognition that we're glad we weren't there. The Johnstown flood. The Columbine shootings. The Watts riots. Three Mile Island. The place I'm

A *note about reality:* Many of the names used in these essays have been changed in order to protect people's privacy. Incidents are as true to actual events as memory and perception allow.

from slips into and out of the public eye, and though we don't remember why, the name Decatur leaves a twinge of dis-ease. . . .

I work in that city and grew up not far from there, in a rural area that feeds its factories. Decatur's been famous three times (so far): first, as a hotbed of labor unrest in 1997; then, in 1999, as the new symbol of racial division; and in 2000 as the producer of self-destructing Firestone tires. Most of the Decatur factories used to be locally owned; hostile buy-outs by multinational corporations changed the delicate labor–business compromises. Strikes by workers at A. E. Staley, Firestone, and Caterpillar were met with repression by the company owners: workers were locked out, and many never returned to their jobs. The employees who remained in these factories often ended up with reduced benefits, twelve-hour shifts, and dangerous working situations. The city is still a pit of animosity, the lingering effects of fired workers versus scabs versus high capitalism.

In the racial incident that brought Decatur its thirty seconds of national attention, six high school students were expelled for two years for fighting at a football game. The scene of a group of young black men chasing another student across outdoor bleachers, shoving aside white spectators, was videotaped by a parent and replayed on TV. Jesse Jackson came down from Chicago to confront the mostly white school board for ending these black students' education. The story was picked up by the wire services, the tape broadcast on national news. The phrase "zero tolerance" entered the public patois. There were demonstrations, speeches, police. Jackson had been a welcomed presence during the labor marches; he helped to build a coalition between white and black workers. But this time, in 2000, his entrance into Decatur was met with cynicism and fear, and with an undercurrent of tentative hope.

I was a child during the '60s Civil Rights marches, barely a teenager when riots flamed the cities. My rural Illinois family was terrified of blacks, but I felt an allegiance with the protesters.

I understood wanting to fight unfairness and violence, because this was what kept the lid of silence on our family and town. By the time I was in high school, I had read *The Autobiography of Malcolm X, Soul on Ice,* and *The Bluest Eye.* I didn't feel like a spectator; I identified. Of course, I wasn't black, and I could never truly understand. But I did know what it was like to stand out because of poverty and troubles. If it was bad for me, then think how it must have been for my friend Rennea, who was from one of the only black families in many country miles.

So when Jesse Jackson came to Decatur and called it Selma, I was interested. The questions of whether six black high school students caused a riot, whether a football game is part of the order of school, whether the almost all-white board is blatantly racist, and whether Jesse Jackson and his entourage should've driven the 250 miles to Decatur were tackled by everyone from the international media to drugstore locals. Few of the African Americans I talked to objected to Jackson's presence—not too surprising—but nearly all of the whites did. Even those who prided themselves on their liberal-mindedness qualified their support of Jackson by wondering whether his involvement was a publicity stunt. The overall white view was that Jackson was interfering in local affairs, making something out of nothing. Most claimed boredom, as if the whole thing were an Oprahcized, phonily dramatic theme show on a "social issue." Plenty were hurt; they felt the city had come a long way in dealing with racial division, especially since the labor strikes. Most didn't care whether the school board did the right thing. They supported the board and waited to see what the Jackson faction—like a dust devil sweeping through town, bringing up debris and dropping it back on the street—would do next.

The whites who *openly* protested Jackson's presence were the scary fringe right-wingers. Central and southern Illinois are breeding grounds for neo-Nazis, the Klan, and assorted militia groups who feel cheated out of their inheritance. Never ones to hide under boulders, the members of the Church of the World Order jumped into the media light. This crew of neo-Nazis is led by skinny, pale, pseudo-intellectual Matt Hale, whose acolyte Benjamin Smith shot up people of darker skin tones in cities across Indiana and Illinois, including Decatur. Hale is a local boy, raised and living in Peoria, and is a graduate of assorted Illinois universities. His beef against Decatur stems from getting kicked out of its symphony orchestra (he's a violinist, as well as the holder of a law degree). His Church of the World Order hit the supermarkets and laundromats and the university where I work with a heavy-duty recruitment drive. Dispensing with old-style maneuvers like marches through town, Hale instead speaks at libraries across the country, which have to let him talk because it's his civil right. The result is a verbal and sometimes physical fight with those who come to protest his speech. Chairs and words are thrown, and Matt Hale gets on TV. The so-called church's cheerful hello and goodbye is "Rahowa!"—Racial Holy War.

Even before Matt Hale's appearance in Decatur came the Klan's, two-hundred strong in a local park. Since I was a kid I've heard murmurings of Klan activity from Galesburg to Cairo. They are particularly strong in the isolated rural areas of western and southern Illinois, where coal mining has declined and un-employment has risen. The hatred of most working-class whites toward any city person telling them what to do is only intensified when that person is black. Insult to injury is how they see it, rubbing their noses in the fact that they are America's bottom-rung losers.

The people least involved in the media-grabbing protests were the kids whose expulsions brought it on. On screen, they looked embarrassed rather than defiant. In print, they noted only their desire to go back to school. Maybe they didn't have Jackson's facility with language; but maybe they didn't know, really, why Jackson was there, didn't understand why they'd been shoved into the national light, why the police trailed them night and day waiting for them to screw up, why their stupid fight became a symbol for school violence and racial discrimination. They were scared and inarticulate high school kids caught doing something wrong, trapped in a situation that went beyond anything they could have fantasized. Printed and photographed, they got lost in the images and forces of a violent action, a white school board, a black activist, and the disembodied voices of a hundred announcers and the typeface of so many newspapers.

The kid who got the most press was Roosevelt Fuller, the football-playing honor student whose life since the fight has turned into a mess. Though Fuller and his friends claimed he was on the sidelines watching the melee, he was kicked off the football team and out of school. Since then, he's been arrested for fleeing the police at a routine traffic stop and for taking a swing at his girlfriend. Ministers and psychologists appeared on talk shows and explained Fuller's plea for help, his anguish at being kept in the spotlight. The black ministers blamed the school board. The board blamed Jackson.

For the country, it was a cross between *Jerry Springer* and *Nightline*. For Decatur, it was history—even Jackson wasn't new. His home base is Chicago, and he's a common political figure in downstate Illinois, where he appears during runs for public office and makes statements about local conflicts. Springfield, the state capital, is only a half-hour's drive from Decatur, and to make things happen in Illinois you have to have a Springfield presence. In the early 1990s during the lockout at the Staley plant, Jackson marched on the side of labor, white and black. His focus, until the school board incident, has been mostly economic, and he maintains close ties to the AFL-CIO. His organizations, the Rainbow Coalition and Operation Push, are funded by major corporations. His interest in the "class gap" makes him a natural in a factory city like Decatur, decimated by union-busting and downsizing. But many of the laborers who embraced him during the strike now condemn him; despite Jackson's insistence that the school board controversy wasn't about race, the reactions of whites proved that it was about just that.

When things get grim in a city, there's going to be fighting. After the lockout of striking workers at A. E. Staley, social analysts predicted a ghost town. It isn't quite, but there is something lost and haunted about the place. Decatur, with all its troubles, has lost 6,000 of its townspeople over the last ten years. It will lose a thousand more now that Firestone is shutting down. Houses are boarded. Blacks and whites hold on to what they've got, try to keep their jobs and move up the line. Racial conflict is personal conflict in a city like this.

Decatur is opaque. What may seem obvious—racism, ignorance, decline, ugliness—is deep and faceted to someone who knows it. Most of the people from Decatur are proud of their city, while they know that, to people driving through, it's a soy-smelly boarded-up roughneck town. It might seem the sort of place that people work hard to leave, except that most residents have lived in this area for generations. They only leave when they can't get jobs.

Decatur survives off of the prairie's bounty. Past the city limits, land extends unobstructed to the horizon. At sunset, silo and home are set off delicately against pink-and-purple skies. Cows, horses, fence posts, and tree branches silhouette in patterns substantial and decorative. Everything has purpose, yet there are moments when a barbed-wire fence seems twisted to lovely ribbons, and when corn leaves curl like a doll's eyelashes. The soil feeds the corn, and the corn feeds the factory and its workers. In Decatur, industries turn corn into feed and sweeteners and oil, and soy into ethanol fuel and vitamin E. The smell of burning organic substances lies over the city in a weirdly syrupy way: some call the smell maple, while others just say it stinks. Folks who live and work in Decatur grow familiar with the stench the way smokers ignore their own second-hand detritus. Some claim it reminds them of home—it's like something cooking, something a lot like people getting fed. The cycle—crops to production to consumption—has kept this area alive for a hundred and fifty years.

This agriculture-to-business routine usually works. People get by without complaint. Unspoken lines are drawn, and we never speak of problems. If the factories lay off, they'll hire again soon—and there are always unemployment checks until they do. If the blacks scare the whites, they're kept out of the white side of the city and the little towns and then forgotten. And, from the black point of view, as long as the whites don't go burning crosses and blocking them from jobs, they can be ignored.

Then something breaks the routine. Demonstrations about race were nothing new to Decatur; smaller, quieter marches riled people up a year before, at Millikin University, the campus where I work. A freshman found her dorm room door scrawled with hate messages. What was written was never openly reported, because the newspapers were too polite to print that most offensive word. The students told me that the messages began with "Go Home, Nigger," and ended with "Leave or Die, Nigger Bitch." The death threat convinced the young woman that it was indeed time to head out. She revealed it to the media, leading to a security lockdown, the rumored presence of the FBI, and press conferences that sent the word out around central Illinois. Nobody was surprised Decatur had racial problems. For whites in the small towns it was bound to happen, simply because the city has a large population of blacks. To the blacks in Decatur it was just one more thing, except that this time it happened within the walls of this cheerful private university instead of on the run-down streets a few blocks from the grassy Millikin hills. To the students, white and black, it was a private fight that had gotten "too blown up."

The dormitory threats happened during my first year at

Millikin, when, fresh out of grad school, I tutored students who struggled with their writing. Most were athletes recruited from Chicago or Decatur. I got to know some of them and we would often move from their sentence structure to what the sentences were talking about: where they came from, their take on the world. I tried to figure out how much writing they'd done, what kinds of schools they'd gone to, so I could relate the putting together of a sentence to the context of their way of seeing. Some knew that this school was their chance to break into the other side: to get a good job, to reach a real dream.

When I asked for their take on the hate messages, maybe they were just being careful. "It's a woman thing," Chris told me. "This girl got it in for her. They know who it is, but they got no proof. Somebody crossed somebody else, that's all." He wouldn't meet my eyes. When I asked Wil, he was even more adamant that "they're taking a little thing and making a big deal out of it. I haven't felt any prejudice. I mean, no more than you get anyplace else." Chris said that he liked the school. "It's red brick. I mean, you look out the window and there are trees. How can anyone not like it?" Others, especially the ones from Chicago, were bored. "Can't we get a Six Flags?" Anthony, a black football player, wrote, "If there was a park, we'd have something to do." No stores, no movie houses. "We're all, like, stuck here with each other," said Renada. "It's like a little boring hick town. And I ain't never gonna be no hick." It wasn't just the African American students who felt this contempt for Decatur and the people who lived there. The suburban Chicago white kids shared the inner city students' attitude, even while most avoided talking to these South Side students. "Decatur's full of freakin' redneck rubes, man," Arnie once said, to loud affirmation by all students except the ones who ducked their heads. When I told him I was from the area, he shut up, but the gleam was still in his eyes.

Yet when Jesse Jackson projected the same view about Decatur, these same suburban kids were quick to label him a hypocritical outsider who needed to get back to Chicago and take care of his own business. When I asked the students in one all-white freshman class whether they felt any association with Decatur, most chimed in with, "Hell, no!" and "Are you kidding? This pit!" and "If they'd burn it down, they might have a real city!" Yet when I asked whether any of them supported Jackson, only one said, "Well, my parents asked me to get his autograph, and I'm going to do it!" Another gave a tentative, "The students really did get a long expulsion. . . ." Like the out-of-towners, the Decatur kids thought the fight was taken out of context. Even if they admitted the existence of racism, they thought the school board controversy had gone too far.

Ron said he'd been at the game. "It wasn't a riot. The guy there filming it, I saw him. He just caught this one little part. They were chasing a guy up and down the bleachers and then these old people almost got run into. We have fights all the time. Eisenhower and MacArthur hate each others' guts." Even in the small school I attended, physical blowups before and after basketball games were common, especially if the schools were rivals. We even had girl gangs who threw punches and pulled hair. Teachers and parents looked the other way, unless property, rather than bodies, was damaged. The difference between these turf wars and the bleacher fight was that all the Decatur kids were black, they were fighting at a public event, and white parents and kids got in the way. Had the fight taken place off the bleachers, it's unlikely that anyone would have noticed or cared. Until Jackson came to town, it looked as if the school board might reach a compromise with the ministers and parents who met to ask for a more reasonable punishment. But once it became public, standing ground became an issue of civic pride.

Brandon, a white student from Decatur, said the whites in Decatur weren't racist, because "the blacks hate me more than I can ever hate them." A musician with scraggly black hair and hunched shoulders, he said that everyone fights everyone. A friend of mine echoed a view I had heard many times, that this incident was part of an ongoing turf war between the Vice Lords and the Gangster Disciples. A 1996 police study of Decatur mentioned the feud, delineating the areas of the city where the criminals were located and discussing details of the drug trade. Gang leaders traveled between Chicago and St. Louis, making lucrative stops in both Decatur and Springfield. A police officer told the press that the fight was a revenge maneuver, caused by one gang member insulting a rival group; the source of that information was the young man who was beaten up.

None of the African American students I talked to thought the fight was drug-related; of course, it's possible that a drug connection wasn't something they'd admit to a white female teacher. Ron said, "At the game, they came right by me, told me they were going to get him, asked if I wanted to go along. I thought about it, but I was busy. Happens all the time." At the college, Ron hung out with a tight group of white and black friends, slackers picking their way between hedonism and scholastic achievement. Ron marched with Jackson and, like the other students who had been there, was struck by the media circus. "They were like a pack, shoving those microphones in his face. I couldn't even see him."

Who the students really noticed were the police. "They had sharpshooters on the roofs, man. Guns pointed, waiting for something to happen." The Decatur police are mostly white, descendants of the Southern Appalachian migration. My cousin is a detective there, and I have distant relatives who work for some of the small-town squads—it can be a protective, reactionary group, suspicious of outsiders.

"Did the police make you nervous?" I asked the guys.

Matt and Evan, the white kids, just looked at each other and shrugged. Ron gave a barely perceptible nod.

"You stay afraid, nothing ever happens," said Matt.

My morning writing class, where I taught this group along

with a cluster of theater and music students, wanted to see Jackson march the expelled students to Eisenhower High School. It was expected that this would be a public demonstration, a show of support, and would take place when the high school opened. They cajoled, and it didn't take much; I told them they could go, but they had to be responsible for themselves. It was their decision, not an assignment. Most went. Two who couldn't find a ride convinced me to drive them in my messy Toyota. I was dubious—I'm on contract at Millikin and didn't want to get fired. But spirits were high and Minni and Geno (a Taiwanese adult student whose real name is Ying-chung) scooted CDs and books off the seats and climbed into my car.

We drove around Decatur's back streets, following a station wagon full of kids from my class. Although I've taught in Decatur for a year and a half, I don't live there—I have kids already in school in another town and don't want to transfer them. I've been past the factories and through one of the poorest areas and over by the cemetery and around the downtown. But Decatur sprawls and turns and there are parts that I've never seen. It's a gray-and-tan city of rundown family businesses and vacant lots. Old brick churches with stained glass line its busiest streets. Tennessee Williams grew up only a hundred miles away, and his depiction of disappointed southern decorum also drifts across the tree-lined streets of Decatur.

I followed that car to Eisenhower High, around blocks of one-story frame houses, each with a porch, a patch of grass with a tree, maybe a rose bush. Instead of jockeys or Madonnas, lawns were littered with plastic daisy whirligigs and cutouts of fat women bent over scraggly flowers. We passed a German shepherd on a chain tied to a stake, and kids' bikes left like wreckage, handlebars to the dirt, tires twisting in the air. A toddler picking up a bug on the sidewalk, a mother staring at us as we passed. It was so quiet on those streets on a workday, in the Midwestern morning mist. "I didn't know this part of Decatur even existed," said Minni. "I've been here a whole semester and I've never been off campus."

"Me either," said Geno, who came all the way from Taiwan to see America. At the stoplight, I glanced back at him. He was reading the jewel box cover of a CD of mine, Mary J. Blige, a black woman's face: *My Life*. Once after class Geno said, in his soft-spoken way, "In America everyone is overly concerned with race." How could I explain, other than to say "yes"? I wish I could've told Geno that in our country race and status don't mean a thing. But that's a lie, though many here will tell you that because teachers and politicians and antisocial malcontents are talking about race and class, we create the division. Did Jackson cause the controversy, as so many people around here say, or did he only bring to light a buried injustice? Or was the school board right in saying that the expulsions had nothing to do with color, that color had become a ploy of blacks wanting attention and excuses? Was the bleacher fight another example of a world spinning out of control, a lack of discipline? Was the board trying to control violence in the only immediate way possible, or were they unfairly choosing who was punished, revealing who was really feared: black males?

Eighty percent of expelled students in central Illinois are black. The residents will tell you that this is because there are more black troublemakers than white. Jackson would say that vicious racism creates a situation in which young black kids fight. The fear of one black man leads to the view that all black men are threats, and this judgment is racism and racism affects self-esteem and economic opportunity. Nothing offended the Decatur school board more than Jackson's assertion, in court documents, that the boys were expelled because of racism. "I am not a racist," the school board president, Kenneth Arndt, pronounced (huffily). No one could see it as a social evil, a twist of perception so deeply ingrained that we barely recognize when it happens. White kids say, in their own defense, that blacks are racist, too: "They don't want to be friends." And sometimes a young white guy will talk about getting threatened or beaten by a black. Like Brandon, the Decatur musician I mentioned earlier. "There's no point in even talking about it," he said. "It is what it is." Granting that, does that make it okay?

All along, I took the stance that I didn't know enough. I hadn't seen the video, hadn't witnessed Jackson firsthand, didn't know the history. Finally, I drove the kids to the march so we could see for ourselves. I'd been to political protests before; as statements of solidarity, gathering witnesses and converts, they feel good. Unlike many of the Decatur residents who saw the marches as an attack on their city, I had no problem with Jackson being there or with his tactics of nonviolent resistance. The skeptical lobe of my liberal brain questioned Jackson's political motives: Was he, as most of my colleagues believed, just using this situation as an opportunity to grandstand for his own gain? Did he take a local conflict that would have been quietly resolved and use it to plaster his face and name across every public medium? Was this emergence during an election year just a coincidence? But Jackson's possible opportunism didn't cancel my own memory of the brutal racism I'd witnessed as I was growing up. I saw what was happening as part of a place that has always been poor and full of fighters. I, too, felt defensive, feeling it was a pity that Decatur made the news, because its blue collar attitude made it easy to skewer when other places were at least as racist. And I felt energized, because in Decatur everything that simmers eventually comes to the surface. Throughout its conflicts, Decatur worked toward harmony as its residents tried to make a place for themselves in an industrial town.

Going to this march, I felt hopeful. Like so many onlookers, we wanted to see an event, but we also wanted to create change. The houses in need of paint, the stores with broken signs showed us that the need was real. I'm doing the right thing, I thought; I want to be here, I want the students to be here.

Closer to the school, we saw people walking. Some parked in a drugstore lot; others left cars on residential side roads. Traffic slowed, then stopped, and down the hill ran a line of vehicles nearly a mile long. A few were waved by police into the school parking lot, but most were barred from turning in.

"They're checking IDs," Minni said. In class, we speculated that they might only let Eisenhower students come near the school. At a four-way stop, and again in front of the school, police waved people forward or to the side. Having students in the car, I got nervous. Trying to avoid the police, I turned onto a side street, still game enough to seek a parking spot and leave it all to fate. Two cops stepped in front of my car.

This well-scrubbed guy barely older than my students grinned at me. "Where you going?"

"I'm a teacher from Millikin. We wanted to observe. My class is writing a paper." This wasn't entirely true, but I thought ingenuousness was best.

He looked at me with kindly pity: you poor head-up-your-ass teacher. "You don't want to be here."

"Really, sir?" I tried to look cute.

"Take my word for it. I don't know what might happen. Things will get bad. You should leave." This was said in a way that I could interpret as advice or as a threat. He peered at the students. And I was afraid. Jackson wouldn't be packing firearms, but the police would. The same Decatur police force had pepper-gassed and arrested Staley strikers only a few years before. Many were recruited from the surrounding rural counties, where the word "nigger" came up so many times in everyday conversation that there was no point telling them they were wrong—because they didn't care if they were wrong. To them, it was survival, protecting what was theirs. I saw this in that policeman's blue eyes.

"Thanks, officer." I turned the car around. "You guys," I told my students, feeling like a coward, "I don't want to be responsible. I don't want you to be there if anyone gets hurt." And I was worried for the others, the students I'd been following and had lost track of at an intersection, and the ones who had gone up a few cars ahead with their old high school passes to Eisenhower. "If it was just me, I'd go." And this was true; I did want to see, and to be on a side. But exposing idealistic private school kids to sharpshooters feeling invaded by Chicago blacks was something I couldn't do.

As it turned out, nothing happened. Jackson, perhaps sensing danger, decided not to approach the school that day and instead talked with the press. The carload of students who'd driven on to Eisenhower saw only backs and cameras; the statement they had hoped to make was silenced by a media opportunity and the city's desire to defuse mass movements. These students had no way in with Jesse Jackson or his camp. They went back to the university and stopped talking about it.

"There's nothing going," Ron said to me a few days later. "It's all TV."

"Pretty pointless, isn't it." And with this statement that was clearly not a question, J.J., savvy, black, and brilliant, put her feet up on her friend's desk as their attention shifted to that evening's party.

CONFIRMATION

"KEEP THESE CHILDREN on the path to the Lord." Pastor Jim, as they called him, walked to the first young person in the semi-circle. Each had gone through weeks of confirmation training and was about to be accepted as an adult in the Lutheran Church. I couldn't see how training prepared anyone for the responsibility of belief or the accidents of fate. The twelve, in black dresses or jackets and white shirts, giggled.

"Do you swear to claim Jesus and let go of the Devil?"

A few mumbles, with one loud and enthusiastic "I do."

"Let's try that one again."

I had missed out on religion. My faith, rooted in woods walks and river musings, had a hard time with social rituals. My faith lay in not buying traditional Christianity. We sat near the back of the church, the contemporary family: husband and wife (parent set one), husband and wife (parent set two), sponsor, grandparents (from parent set two, or us, Doug and me). I played the role of newly added second wife, which was harder than just being a wife.

The history: Four years ago, Doug's ex fell back in love with her old high school boyfriend. The hurtful divorce involved itemized lists of belongings for an equitable split. But what's fair in ex-love? Doug ended up with the house, and, months later, me; she got her guy and the furniture and cash. The kids, his and mine, bounced back and forth while everyone tried to be responsible. Rituals and patterns became family glue: the choir concert, rides from school, taking the dogs to get their shots. Church was part of this.

This wasn't the church where Doug and I sang, the only one I'd attended as an adult. Ours had stained glass and a rowdy white choir. This house of worship, the ex's, was a kind I'd never gone to before. It made me want to get outside—how could any entity be praised in a dark room? The place had padded chairs instead of pews (or fallen logs), contemporary songs instead of hymns (or bullfrog croaks), and the pastor's haranguing sermon. "We must accept change," he yelled. "Change is inevitable. Change is the next day. Change is happening right now." Bad homilies, except the minister got stirred up like a Sunday morning TV preacher: "And GAWD said we must follow the lamb UNLESS we want to live a life of SUFFERING and find ourselves BURNING in the flames of HELL." Social control by guilt, like some old Marxist said; maybe, like me, everyone counted sins instead of blessings. Turned out the pastor was worked up because he was raising money for a new church. Change was financial and ascendancy demanded cash.

Church meant fitting in, sharing a place, admitting the rightness of being with others. Like the transcendentalists and the Native Americans, I saw belief as a personal spirit quest, a wondering. Organized religion emphasized the bargain of accepting what we were told, so that the world would hold together. I wanted to fit in, too. The fact that church hadn't always been a part of my life, the way it was to these Lutherans, felt lonely. I needed to comprehend the normalcy of their ritual, to offhandedly know when to confess, kneel, commune.

Before marrying Doug, I'd had only a two-year stint in a tiny rural church in Buffalo, Illinois. My parents refused to go. We moved from dry, rambling Phoenix to that backwater Illinois town when I was in third grade. My mom struggled to handle her brother's death from a brain tumor and my dad's erratic outbursts. She was in no mood to have her soul saved at the white frame church a few blocks from our house.

Age nine, I sat at the formica-top kitchen table working to convince her that church was fun, that people were nice. I walked to Sunday school classes alone, sometimes staying for services; I loved the songs and stories about Jesus. I wanted my parents to stand among the grown-ups who clustered in the entryway, sharing greetings and friendly gossip. Grandma watched as I tried to tempt them into religion. She dropped sugar cubes into her coffee, wearing her usual look of reserved amusement. "Why not, Mom?" I wheedled, not understanding her refusal to leave the house. Day after day, she sat in the dark, avoiding everyone except Grandma and her sister, Teresa. Rather than go out, she'd send me to the town's grocery store and post office. Our house on Wells Street was small and had few windows, except in the kitchen where we often sat. Her hours were spent ironing and watching *As the World Turns* and *The Edge of Night,* sprinkling water onto the clothes from an old Coke bottle with a shaker top. When the Welcome Wagon lady came by—Mrs. Shanle, wife of the town's only insurance agent—Mom took the basket full of apples and nuts and politely shut the door. Invitations to block parties, the PTA, and American Legion dances all went unheeded.

"These society people think they know so much," Mom said of the Welcome Wagon woman in her lavender skirt and high heels. She said the same thing of the church. "It's only a place where people go to show off their clothes and prove how good they are. They get blessed, then go home and do what they're not supposed to."

"The rich people sit up front so everyone will see them," added Grandma, who was Catholic and wanted to be a nun before she married Grandpa. She had gotten tossed around as a child, from an orphanage to a mean aunt in Chicago who made her dust the chandeliers (or so went the family story). In between, she stayed with her father who ran rum during Prohibition and had an assortment of wives. That Grandma fell in love with a bullshitting-but-responsible rogue was no surprise. Instead of a habit, she wore cut-off blue jeans, a gingham blouse, and her black hair in a French twist that strayed free of its clips. She only went to Mass on Christmas. Yet, serene and content, she'd found the center of herself while the cows and trees flew in the whirlwind around her.

I didn't understand why Mom was so offended by church. Nobody there seemed to notice me. I sat in the back beside my friend Debbie and listened to stories of disciples and loaves and crumbling towers and felt lifted above everything around me. The people disappeared in the light that came through the simple stained glass.

CONFIRMATION

21

I'm not sure if it was paranoia, jealousy, or comprehension that made my mom get mad about my Bible. A week after I'd been pestering her to come to church, she found it on my dresser. "What, they think we're too poor to buy you one?" she ranted, though, yes, we were too poor. My dad had gotten on at Firestone in Decatur, so every afternoon he disappeared carrying a silver lunchbox (he worked graveyard every third week, and three-to-eleven on others). We existed on soup beans and Kraft macaroni and cheese, with maybe carrot sticks or a plain salad of head lettuce on the side. Mom never considered working; women in my family did not have jobs once the children came. It was so taboo that it was never discussed, though Mom was smart and bored and bitter and we could have used the income. "Do they think we need charity?"

"No," I mumbled. "She just wanted me to read it." It was a present from my school teacher, Mrs. Walker, who had only half an index finger. While singing "Jesus Loves Me," I used to stare at the puckered pink stump, which looked like the end of a hot dog. She waved it in rhythm to the music, and licked it before turning the page of the cartoon Bible story. A full-color anemic Jesus smiled beatifically from behind her hand. Mrs. Walker was a kindly, patient, plump woman who smelled of cooked cabbage, and I was shyly pleased to have gotten the Bible.

"Don't talk back to me." Mom's black hair hung like drapery around a long, olive-skinned face. She scared me, but I was determined to never let her know it and reacted with blank face and obstinate silence. Her breath smelled of cigarettes and coffee, and I kept out of arm's reach. On the best of days we weren't a huggy, touchy family.

"Never take handouts," she warned, though she didn't make me take back the Bible. Instead, she went into the kitchen and rattled the dishes. I know now how much she hated leaving the Arizona sun, hated burying a brother she'd spent her life protecting and caring for (he'd had juvenile arthritis), hated slinking home to bum money off her parents. But I doubt the churchgoers knew about my mother's comedown; they lived in a dinky town, miles from anything, and were hardly rolling in cash. Everyone had a sin; that was why they went to church.

I kept going alone. I'd turn the pages of the free Bible comic books telling of miracles and disasters. I believed in Jesus' philosophy of gentle generosity, turning the other cheek, live and let live. Passivity and silence were not only okay, but also states of blessedness, and this proved that I was a good person. Looking through my black Bible, I learned all the books of the Old and New Testament by heart. I wore a cross, plastic with a rose inside, which I'd bought with my own money at the State Fair. I felt like that rose and believed that the clear hard plastic was my secret protection, the way belief protected all Christians from the ambiguous dangers in their dreams.

Grown at last, having a kid dislodged the loner in me; teachers, other parents, and many children walked in and shook my reflective withdrawal. My world became set in child ways; stories that melded my mom and grandma and aunt over coffee became the ones I shared with school parents. I never forgot how different I'd felt as a kid walking to church by myself while families pulled to the curb in newly washed Oldsmobiles. I had distracted myself by looking up at the leaves and listening to the mourning doves, and while my loneliness was imaginative and bittersweet, it wasn't what I wanted for my daughter. I wanted to be with my kids, even if I couldn't do it gracefully. I had to give to gain, and give up to gain. Though this was a Christian attitude, I hoped it wasn't merely a trade-off for brownie points in Heaven. It was selfish, really. The children became the parameters of my life, and this made it easy to sit in the pew.

When the pastor at my stepson's confirmation told us, though, that Jesus was a harsh judge, I got pissed. People who made mistakes or tumbled into accident—taking drugs, getting AIDS—were fallen and condemned, he said, and so worthy of our forgiveness. I was horrified at the presumption that anyone

CONFIRMATION

23

in that congregation could be superior simply because they were more fortunate. Maybe Mom's fears were founded; we would have been pitied and ridiculed if the good Christians had witnessed the poverty of our emotional and financial lives. They would have wanted to redeem us. To forgive me, the child. I believed in innocence. Actions might need mending through better ones, but I couldn't accept a broad, nameless sin. Children weren't born with guilt, nor did they need the sanction of a formal religious baptism. If everyone was damned, then how could any good effort make any real difference? With such an easy notion of forgiveness, how could there be responsibility for an imperiled world? If prayers wiped away the blame for the destruction of our earth, our cruelty to other people, and if there were by default those who were "bad" on the basis of stupid, blameless error, then what action was truly moral?

I had asked my questions to the trees many times and had found more definitive answers than I would ever get in church. Which wasn't to say I didn't do wrong things. I wasn't Saint Rebecca of the Flowers, a nun, an angel, or even a good singer. Every wrong stayed a weight, and hope lay only in the forgiveness of those who cared and in my own forgiveness of myself. I made horrible mistakes, but so did everyone, and this made us flawed and human. Jesus understood that one; maybe he walked on water, but he was also a man. He knew Mary Magdeline; had he been a woman, perhaps he would have been her.

In trying to understand my losses, a time came when I talked to Jesus at the river. Well, I didn't know I was talking to Jesus; I was really talking to the river, which was spirit. It was only a matter of definition to me then, at twelve. Blessings were iffy notions; what was taken for granted could be quickly snatched away. As a child, I delivered secret wishes in paper folded tightly over and over, creased until the wish was a box of itself and could become no smaller. I would ask for a paperback book or for my mother to be happy. But mostly I wished for my uncle to come back from the dead.

here and now in soy city

And I asked him to once, during a Ouija séance I held with my cousins and my brother. This was after Dad got a new job at the hospital in Springfield. My family left the little town of Buffalo and moved to a house on my grandparents' few acres. Backcountry in Illinois, the slope on the land next to ours rose up, and on top of it was a round cement well cover, smooth except for a few nicks, as if someone had struck it with a hammer. We kids sat on the hot slab. Our shorts, cut from old jeans, were so high in the legs that our thighs burned, one side from the concrete and the other from the sun. Playing in the house was futile; we had no air conditioning and our basement floor, which was our kitchen floor, was so damp with humidity that our feet left imprints. Better to be where a breeze stirred the ash trees. From the hilltop we could see the river, the Sangamon, not far below, moving slowly, low from lack of rain.

My brother Tony didn't want in the game; his mind never stayed on one thing. He wanted to build a pit that would house a hideous gravel monster. This hole would be like the one down the road from our house from which trucks emerged spilling rocks across our blacktop and cracking windshields of all who traveled behind them.

"Oh, fine, go," I said, though I figured the more hands, the more melded minds, the better chance of my plan's success. I'd been reading mystical books, Edgar Cayce and Colin Wilson, and I knew that thoughts set toward the supernatural could make things happen—good and bad and indifferent. We could conjure the dead, especially those uneasy watching spirits like my uncle. The in-between place where I imagined him held infinite goodness and understanding, and he hung out there with fellow ghosts keeping an eye on things. He wasn't gazing down; his feet were on the ground, or at most no higher than the treetops.

So Tony went off, a small silver airplane in his hand, and with him went my littlest cousin, Joey, frail and shy with buzz-cut hair.

CONFIRMATION

That left my cousins Mike and Brenda. And a cardinal pecking around in the grass, a female and so not as proud and bright as the male. I took her as a sign. Not like Poe's raven; the only birds like that were the evil jays that stole other birds' eggs right from the nest. My redbird was a good omen, an emissary and watcher who would report back like an angel.

I was a believer in signs. Something was coming, a wind blowing against my spread fingers. Our summers were so long and hot and silent that it was easy to hear the rustlings of change that for city people were hidden beneath the squealing of tires and rush of feet on pavement. I didn't know its substance, only that it signaled my connection with something more significant than myself.

Maybe it was my uncle. He'd been gone six years. I slept in the bedroom he had when he came back to Illinois to live with my grandparents before he died of a brain tumor. His crucifix, a tan Jesus splayed across a tan cross, hung in the room. It spooked me, but it seemed wrong to take it down. From that crucifix my uncle's spirit made its entrance during many long nights, not floating like in some movie, but diffuse and permeable, motes scattered above my bed. I wanted the pieces to come together, so it would be the way it was in Phoenix when he taught me how to paint, before my life was filled with Midwestern trees and a too-bright yellow room.

My cousin Mike wasn't going for it. Then again, he barely remembered my uncle. Five years younger than me, Michael was a wise kid who knew just who he was. He knew he was right and had no need to argue. He was curious about the séance, but didn't believe. I could tell because he wasn't saying anything, a sure sign he thought something was stupid. But the pull of age was on my side; he'd ride along in case I knew something he didn't.

"Let me see that thang." Like me, he said "lemme," and "whar," and "ain't got no." We twanged like Appalachian fiddles, though two hundred miles north was this huge city, Chicago. But that was another world for as close as we were going to get to it.

Mike held the Ouija doohickey, white plastic with a blue, not-quite-transparent center. "Looks like nothin'," he said, plopping it in the center of the board.

"I wanna play." Brenda, sweet and adaptable, wore a brown dress with a bow around her neck. She wasn't allowed to wear pants, even though it was 1970 and every other girl in America lived in jeans. She grabbed the marker and aimed it at the scripted letters on the cream-colored board. "S-I-S-S-Y," she said, "Sissy," because that was what we called her, Sis, or Sister.

Her brother ripped it out of her hand. "D-U-M." Mike darted the pointer from letter to letter.

"Hey!" Brenda didn't know what it spelled, but knew it had to be bad, and they arm-wrestled until I yelled, "Stop! Cut it out! This is serious!" They looked at me in mid-struggle, and, seeing that I meant it, Brenda said, "Fine, then," and folded her arms, and with a sweep of politeness Mike put the marker back on the board.

"Show us what you're up to then." With his finger, he poked at the ridge of his gum where his front tooth was starting to come in. His skin, like mine, looked like an undusted bookshelf from playing out in the sand. Dirt in sweat left a shine, because we didn't often take baths in the summer (unless we were going into town, maybe once a week).

He was the only one in the family with eyes of hazel or green, depending on the light and the time of day. He was everlastingly patient with me, since I was erratic and ethereal while he was solid as clay. Reassured that he'd go with me on this spirit trek and help me get back, I placed my fingertips on the Ouija marker.

"We must close our eyes," I intoned. "Breathe and contemplate. If we believe, he will appear." I wanted to ask a question, but didn't know one. I just wanted my uncle to be there.

The books said spirits knocked beneath tables and blew out candles and caused breezes to swoosh through dead-silent rooms. I wanted to know that someone was watching. To have proof that I wasn't in it alone.

Their eyes were closed. "Think hard," I said, "and he'll appear." My mind was set to steely certainty, to direct conduit. Come here, be here, think of me, visit. After awhile, I forgot all but my chant—my cousins, the wind, even the plastic marker that gave my fingers a place to rest.

When the calling gave way to a pained and lonely waiting, I opened my eyes. My cousins stared, and they might have been everyone I ever knew, and I wondered what I had given away. Had my lips moved? Had I cried? Said words, believed too hard—no one, ever, was supposed to be serious, so vulnerably transparent. I looked behind, to the river, thinking he would be there, or some of him. But nothing had changed; not so much as a breeze shifted the leaves. I prayed the marker had moved even one letter. But it hadn't.

The hair stuck to my damp temples. I wanted to scratch my knee, something normal like that, but all I could do was know that he was gone for real. Any movement might make someone laugh. I could see it in my cousins' faces. Mike pulled his hand from the marker and stretched.

"Well. That was fun," he yawned.

The game piece was light, a manufactured toy. "It's moving," I whispered, in the most dramatic, awestruck voice I could muster. "H-E-L-" I made it go fast for the big effect. "L-O," I called out, "see there! He said hello!"

"Wow," sighed Brenda, bouncing on her knees.

Mike, the realist, looked at my hand and snickered. "Yeah."

"Isn't that something, Bren?" I said. "He really was here."

"Really. . . ," she intoned, in her five-year-old ability to believe what was in front of her eyes. "Magic."

"Goodbye," said Mike, and he hightailed it down the hill to where my brother pushed Tonkas in the sand.

"Let's say more." It was a game, the kind I always used to

entertain my cousins, and I made it go. If I believed, then it was true, and if I didn't believe, I could make it happen anyway. It was a matter of the right words. The cardinal had flown away and come back, and no trucks passed on the blacktop. A hush and the leaves in the highest branches shook all around.

Thirty years later, standing near an altar, I sent my stepson on his lonely venture into a grown-up world. If he believed, as he claimed, then I wondered what would make him doubt—or if he doubted already, what with the way his friends giggled and the pastor intoned obedience and sacrifice and basic church fundraising. What did this slight, sullen thirteen-year-old wish for? His old family, his less complicated, pre-divorce life? Was he happy having four parents standing with him instead of two? When he asked for an answer, what did he hear?

He wasn't telling. Prayers aren't Ouija, but a request can be a prayer. When my parents moved out of the little town and I couldn't go to church, I took my wishes downstream. The evening after the séance I went out alone and stared into the river. The sky was pink-streaked indigo and the birds and insects noisy and restless. I scrambled down the steps dug into the bank until I was near the water. On a jutted and muddy stretch of sand, I picked up rocks worn smooth by currents. When I threw, they hit with definitive ploonks, spreading circles that radiated along the silver sundown water. I got artful. Using flatter rocks, I curved my arm for the throw, going for the skip, skip, skip. Like the dragonfly that flitted over the surface of the water, the skimming bug doing the butterfly stroke with eyelash legs, questions and answers were pointless; being was simple. My uncle had been there all along. No bad fortune, no doubts changed the irrefutable fact that I propelled the skipping stone and the water buoyed it across. And when the rock disappeared, the river kept on, and the stone was there with the others, until it would someday make its way to shore.

CONFIRMATION

CLAIMING SOY CITY

SOYBEANS. The smell hangs thick over Decatur, like a lollipop left to melt on a heat register—sweet and sticky and almost nauseating. Locals are used to this: the scent of money, Archer Daniels Midland, jobs. Midwestern and rural as corn, soybeans are fillers in ice cream and gasoline. Soybeans balance menopausal women and lubricate machinery. They grease our lives, and in return Decaturites work to get those products moving.

Decatur aspires to little, not even alteration. Strikes, layoffs, and transfers keep the community in a state of unpredictability. Houses are boarded; thefts are common. Like anywhere, depressants remove the edge. African Americans and whites live in separate pockets and everyone is scared. Decatur is the only truly grimy city in a central Illinois rectangle: Champaign-Urbana (U of I, intellectual), Bloomington-Normal (ISU, State Farm Insurance, button-down), and Springfield (Illinois government, land of payoffs). Decatur, with its stench, violence, and decline, sits like a hunkered-down dog in the midst of professional prosperity.

I've come to this town to teach. I know this stretch of territory as thoroughly as I remember the footholds of my old climbing tree. My dad worked graveyard at Decatur's Firestone factory for three years. Much later, I had a sweet boyfriend, the son of a preacher, who lived in a boxy Decatur bungalow. Driving into town from Bloomington where I live an hour away feels solid, familiar, like home.

My job is at a private college that caters to the children of small towns and inconsequential cities. Millikin is an oasis of prettiness in roughneck turf of billboards, bowling alleys, and liquor stores. The students hate Decatur, and fights between them and the townies are common: greasers versus pretty boys, jocks versus guys at the bar, gays versus gay bashers. A lot of the students are the first in their families to go to college, which means they aren't much different from the locals—except that their parents did a little better, had the savvy to know the value of a private education, and raised kids who scored okay on their ACTs. The kids' folks moved to the country or the suburbs to protect themselves from the multiple colors and conflicts of cities like Decatur. The students know they're on their way. What do the townies have to look forward to but lives assembling parts, or telling people how to assemble parts?

When I come into my 12:30 class, there's Arnie, a funny, very blond football player with a chest like a wall. Arnie and Hanson are the hotdogs in a class of giggly-but-smart female nursing students, and they're doing star turns. "We got that guy drunk and then took him out in the fields and left him there."

"Arnie! Please don't tell me you did a thing like that"; "That's mean," sigh the women, with a disapproving finger-shaking tone: those cute boys, beating somebody up again.

"It was just one of the stupid Decatur freaks we met downtown. One of those slimy bucktooth types—"

"Gawd, Arnie!" says Christine, showing real offense.

"He would've done the same to us."

"Hey, wait, I'm from Decatur." Lil has a made-up, artificially smiling face and a cheerful attitude, but underneath there's this anger.

"Yeah, you're one of those idiots who goes to the factory every day," Hanson teases. He's showing off; his papers talk about how much he loves the trumpet and loves women, and every day he gets a new earring or a few more spikes in his hair. The young women call Hanson "creative."

Lil stands on the seat of her desk. (Well, class hasn't officially started; I haven't set down my papers.) "Listen, buster, I'll have you know that people in this town know how to work—"

"You're stupid, Hanson," says Lil's friend Carole.

"Look, this guy was just asking to get tossed." Arnie crosses his massive arms over his chest. "He was calling us names, he was sloshed, and you know there was that fight last week."

"That doesn't mean you have to behave that way, too," says Lil.

"Greaser," Hanson accuses.

here and now in soy city

32

"Snob," sniffs Lil. She sits in her seat and looks at me.

"Is there a lot of this stuff going on?" I ask.

All the time, I'm told. The locals hate us; the soybeans stink; I was followed by a man in a car; we're trapped with nothing to do; when we go out, all we take is crap; everyone in this town is ignorant and illiterate. I don't like the city, anyway. This town is too small; I'm from Chicago. I'm bored. They'd like to kill us.

My dad stayed at Firestone until he got a better dead-end job controlling a hospital's boilers. The sound of the machines was so loud, at whatever his jobs, that there was no point in trying to talk. Even the booth where he adjusted dials wasn't soundless enough to escape the hum and vibration. He doesn't hear people now, out of physical deafness and, I guess, from giving up trying to listen.

Some of these students would label this a white trash existence. I see it as necessity, acceptance, acquiescence.

On his way home from Firestone, Dad would stop at the gas station and buy us candy. Necco wafers, SweeTarts. For himself, Wrigley's clove gum (which I would swipe off his dresser). In his silver lunchbox was some junk novel, a bad adventure or something dirty that I wasn't supposed to see. He'd read these books when he wasn't checking the dials. He also brought home this magazine put out by the UAW. The union ran notices about never buying Zero and Hollywood candy bars. Aggressive, outraged, these warnings against chocolate were mysterious to me at nine; manufacturers were committing horrible atrocities and the good guys, working men like my dad, were out to stop it. Dad would tell me to pay no attention. "They're stirring up trouble. They need to shut up and do their jobs." His position at Firestone wasn't unionized, because he wasn't a line worker.

While he was at the plant, there was a strike.

In my classroom on another day, the students talk about labor. A fourth of the class has parents who had been laid off or on strike at factories in Decatur, Peoria, and some of the smaller Illinois towns (Lincoln, Mt. Pulaski, Illiopolis, Mason City, . . . so many names for black dots on the map). We watched the movie *Roger and Me* in which muckraker Michael Moore nails General Motors for destroying Flint, Michigan, when the factories closed. I thought it might put them in a rebellious mood.

"My dad was out on strike for two years," says Erin. "But it wasn't so bad. He just did work on the side, started a little business. You make do, you know?" She shrugs.

"So they left Flint and went on to jobs out west," says Arnie. "What's wrong with that?"

"My mom got laid off at Caterpillar," says Leslie.

"Gary, Indiana, is a creepy ghost town," throws in Renada, one of the few African Americans in my class.

"If the factories left, our whole town would be gone."

"Half our town did move out."

"I don't understand why they have to whine about it, though."

"GM is out to make money. That's the way it is. That's the American way."

"You just get on with your life."

The rules: Work hard. Never take handouts. Don't talk about your problems. Don't stir up trouble. No complaints.

My dad crossed picket lines. He never protested a thing, but anger over who he was and where he was stuck made him crazy. Growing up in frigid Minnesota at the end of the Depression, he and his brother stole potatoes off boxcars. His father, gassed in World War I, was too sick to work. His mother, Maud, a religious fanatic, banned dancing and apparently everything else. Dad and his brother quit high school to fight in the Korean war. Dad became a sergeant and came through it convinced that he really didn't like people. His brother was killed.

Dad was a war hero; he saved, a book says, two hundred men. He has nightmares, seizures, and violent rages, and flies the flag on a pole outside his house. A member of the VFW, he was furious not at being sent to Korea, but at the government, which "didn't let us finish what we'd started." The men in my family

here and now in soy city

believed that war protesters should be shot; saying no was morally wrong. People must follow their duty; anything else was a threat to "everything us vets worked for."

So Dad crossed a picket line, and my students in Decatur think Michael Moore is a freak for bothering the poor president of General Motors. The workers of Flint, they say, should get back to work. Those who live off welfare and unemployment meet with their deepest contempt.

"Lazy and stupid," Hanson sums up. "Losers."

"Just like those guys downtown. You know, how they walk around in their dirty coats all day talking to themselves."

"Schizophrenics?" I say.

"Yeah. Fruit loops."

Some of the kids shake their heads. But they are afraid to walk off campus, afraid to enter the poverty-hit community surrounding their red brick enclave. One young woman, doing an internship at the Y, wears pepper spray around her neck. She was tailed by a van of men who yelled at her to get in until she got to the island of mown grass. Then they drove beneath the graffiti-scarred overpass that umbrellas Oakland Street. She still looks for them to come back.

At the gas stations near the university, cashiers are protected behind bulletproofed glass. Compare this with the chatty family service stations in the little towns, where the bored men gossip and the young guys rev their cars. Even the Chicago kids, most of them, are from neighborhoods of friends and family. Kept on the campus, they feel trapped, though they also say of the school, "It's just like a town," a tiny community of like people.

The Decatur townies threaten all that students wish to become: successful, and nothing like where they came from. They credit their grades and talents for getting them out of the neighborhood, the backwater highway stop. Yet they are terribly homesick.

Millikin was built on a graveyard, and students tell of hauntings. Ryan claims that the ghost in his room turns on the

TV, causes the phone to ring, and eats SpaghettiOs. There's even a book about the ghosts, who are victims of fires and suicides. The school is surrounded by a cemetery, a park, and streets leading to bars and dry-cleaning stores and the mansion of James Millikin, founder of the school. At the university, music from dance and vocal classes drifts across the bricked quad. Beyond, the town is worn, but it maintains the character of an old southern city; the downtown stores reside in turn-of-the-century buildings. The lack of money for urban renewal has allowed the declining to remain, giving Decatur an atmosphere that upscale apartment buildings have destroyed in other cities. The students aren't old enough to appreciate, say, the bar where locals gather to tip beers, soothed by TVs and dark wood and fried mushrooms. They want a dance bar, a sports bar; they want a mall and a Cineplex and a water park.

I like Decatur's sense of trapped time, its embrace of tradition, dialect, roots. The locals think the students go too far—they are envious of those at the college, but they also pity us. In our drive to get over, the planting stops; time speeds up; we lock our pets in generic apartments, and no deer, raccoons, or mice come to our urban yards for food; we don't know our neighbors. Our lives constrict like the university, turning inward with ideas, and we reject the world that brought us there, and become ashamed of it and of them. When the children go, the community crumbles. As blacktop expands into highway, the townies see the end of their road.

"The old friends all act supportive," says Chris, a smart African American who played football for Stephen Decatur High. "But they really be lookin' to stick a knife in your back." This is the same Chris who said that getting an education would get him out—that, and his ability to run a ball. Only by excelling physically and mentally did he see himself as having half a chance of beating out the white kids. "The folks at home just wantin' to pull you back in, back down," Chris says.

The students visit home, commuting down the Decatur

streets lined with donut shops and liquor drive-thrus until hitting the back roads. The run-down city makes them eager for chain stores. Until you get to Decatur's single mall, there's one worn family business after another. Mom-and-Pop cafés squat next to Quikie-Marts. Used car lots lurk across from easy-loan storefronts. Square brick multi-storied houses snuggle in pockets of relative wealth; professors live in slow-moving neighborhoods where tree branches drape over sidewalks. Heat, combined with the factory smell that goes beyond soy into something palpably greasy, creates waves leading to somnolence. A house with beveled glass and a turret goes for nothing compared to what it would cost in an upscale city. Subdivisions sprout along highways, in incorporated areas with hopeful names, as commuters avoid Decatur proper. My cousin Joe lives in one of these; a cop, he's seen enough drug busts and battered women to grow tired before the age of thirty. Their home is far from the tense seediness that comes once the highway turns into Eldor-ado, the busy street leading through rows of gray block buildings and plastic signs with missing letters.

When Dad worked nights at the Firestone factory on that same Eldorado, we kids moved around the house as silently as we could; we didn't want him stumbling out of the bedroom in his underwear, angry and exhausted. While we played outside in our small-town bliss of garden, trees, and lanes, we had to be careful not to call out beneath his window.

Factory grit infected our house; not real dirt, but an annoyance under the nails, nagging and biting, that legacy of a worthless night and a day slept through. Dad hated Decatur, and my mother hated that little house in that town of three hundred on the stretch of pitted Highway 36; Dad cursed that highway as a sheet of ice in winter, a corridor for speeders in summer. Decatur was everything to avoid, as it is for the students; according to Dad, it was filthy, full of black people (said as the expected curse), and a long, dull drive.

I travel a different highway: 51, a four-lane separated by a swatch of green, set in stark farmland. Gold, green, brown in patches and textures: furrows, hills, waves, and silken flatness. A mist rises from the ground some mornings, settling into hollows, rising beside a creek or deep ditch. Fires spark beyond the field, burning brush, the flames rising high while nearer the road a stallion mounts a mare. Deer gather close to the highway, fearless in pursuit of food; and although the roads of Illinois are littered with their carcasses, it's still a surprise to see them in the daylight. Above are prairie birds: geese vee-ing toward a fishing lake, swallows rising out of the fields in some startled realization of freedom. A pheasant walks jut-legged and ragged-feathered in the ditch; an owl, entranced, stares from a fence post. Narrow, straight Highway 51 is a seam in the countryside, not a jagged tear that poisons with noise and exhaust, and the car is the means to a specifically American adventure. The drive is my statement of independence as I defy semitrailer truckers, my mother's cautions against traveling alone, and my inhibitions about new territory. For Dad, the drive meant entering a trap, something he had to do to support a family he didn't want. For me, it's a route to the place where I can support my family with a few ideas and in return gain the energy that comes from stirring it up with young people. I never forget my luck—I could have ended up pushing paper or parts in the factory.

Yet on days when I'm tired of grading, I become the factory worker. Seeing a student, I slap on that patient smile and then teaching feels like other droning, draining jobs I've had, like bagging hospital trash, mopping floors, stamping envelopes, typing pages and pages of the boss's illegible handwriting. The difference is that I want the university. Nobody chooses a laborer's job; you are selected by circumstance. This is why the locals hate the students.

My parents were never content, but they were content to not change. They taught me never to give up a good paying job. I did. I went to New York, I went to colleges, I chased down various dreams and killed them, coming back to that Illinois highway like the one my father used to drive. It was harder than escape and feels like achievement, for in claiming home and reaching equanimity, I've nearly conquered my family's furious discontent. Home is possessed upon my own terms. My brick building, book-strewn office, overpass, cement sidewalk to the decrepit donut shop: workers built them, and I'm a worker, controlling everything produced by my hands. I know we don't all labor together, and the university is, as one friend called it, a jewel in a sewer—but I can't stop feeling that my hand works the pen much in the same way that my uncle's worked a hammer. I like the lady who passes the cinnamon roll at the coffee shop. I like to watch history. Am I like my relatives, working with hands and heart? Yes. No. Yes. No!

When my mother died, the visitation was held at the funeral home in the same small town where she'd grown up. I'd been there before. The director of the funeral home knew everyone in my family from other visits. "Your family is always fighting," he laughed to me. He means Family, scattered across Decatur and Springfield and towns in between. (Nobody leaves Illinois.) I met Family at the funeral who I'd never even heard of. One came up to me and shook my hand. I smiled as I'd been smiling all night. I'd been so busy smiling that I'd hardly had time to look at the urn and the flowers.

This man, a salesman, asked me about myself. This was important, how we kids ended up. I told him I worked at Millikin.

"As a secretary?"

"No, I teach there."

"You mean, you hold some fifth grade classes there or something."

"No. I'm a professor. I teach writing and American Studies to college students."

Shock crossed the man's face and he was suddenly all over

himself being impressed. I laughed, but I had one of those moments of real confusion. Connie Bradway's daughter a professor? That was the attitude. I don't think he entirely believed me. I'm not sure *I* believed me.

It's just persistence, I want to say. It's my mother's stubbornness, my father's rage. The possibility of education. But among those country people in that funeral home, I realized again that I had moved far from home.

Someone once asked me why I never broke away. It was because I didn't want to. I like corn. I like the openhearted students. I embrace history. History doesn't care.

THE LANGUAGE
OF GRACE

I SIT IN THE BACK ROW, knowing I have to leave early. The church opens out like a fan, pews arrayed with those who wait to absorb the choir and get religion. Scattered among blacks like spilled sugar are teachers and parents of the few white singers. The Caucasians look uncomfortable but hopeful, lips drawn together, excited at their children's performance. The African American parents seem the most content, because they know what's going to happen, the language is theirs. They are dressed formally in black and blue and red, silks and polyester suits, heels in which they can stride. This isn't a student presentation, but a crossing.

I come because I have been asked. Because I'm curious. I teach across the street from the church that allowed this performance to take place. My students asked me to come so I could see what it is that they do best. I watch the way I would a movie about a culture I've never visited, a place romantic, exotic, a little scary. I shouldn't feel this separation, but most whites don't grow up living near black families; meetings, if they happen at all, tend to take place in public places, like school or the mall. Where I went to secondary school, only a half hour away from this church, there were no blacks; at the colleges that taught me, very few. More than thirty years have passed since I had a close African American friend I could talk to about everything that matters. My best black friends now are Africans who hold onto their citizenship to other countries, reluctant to officially join this one. It's easier to find an African working in higher education than an African American. Most quit before they get a B.A., let alone a Ph.D. More quit, I imagine, than poor whites, although it's hard to find *anyone* who teaches college who'll admit to growing up poor. Hiding class background is a matter of choice; the goal is to climb the ladder and leave all that behind. We can lose ties and history. Nobody leaves race.

The group singing is the Multicultural Voices of Praise, a university choir that draws from a spectrum of faiths. As

43

the nave fills with blacks, I feel uneasy. Not about them (I don't think), but about whether I'm transgressing—and whether this is the day the neo-Nazis or the Klan makes a move. A few days before, the Church of the World Order, an Aryan nationalist group, held a counter-demonstration to protest a march organized by Jesse Jackson's Operation Push. When Jackson protested the zero tolerance policy in the local school—a policy that appeared to single out black males—Decatur, Illinois, was blasted across the airwaves. This, in turn, has attracted every right-wing group hungry for attention. In the media, the debate shifted from its core battle—racism—into rules surrounding school violence. Here everyone knows what the fight is really about: tensions between working-class whites and blacks in this Midwestern small-town-grown-to-city, and the appearance of a national figure in a place that hunkers in its own local affairs. It's not the African Americans in town who are violently angry; they're just calling attention to an old problem. It's the whites, furious with the humiliation of being exposed on national television. The two-year expulsion of six black kids for fighting at a football game is a private matter, they say. Like a bar fight, or hitting a child with a board, or firing a malcontent. The way it's always been.

Some of the students in this choir marched with Jackson. Some are from Chicago, trying to make their transplanted adjustment to a downstate oasis that isn't, for them, protected. Others grew up in Decatur, the working-class town surrounding the college. They're outsiders on the campus, too. Never admit you're from Soy City, land of Archer Daniels Midland, Staley, and Caterpillar. Nobody puts up with more degrading comments than Decatur's "ghetto blacks" and "trailer trash" whites. Many in the choir hang onto classes by C's. Some will flunk out, and not because they're stupid. They just can't keep it organized. Their alarm clocks delay, they hang out too long in the halls. They don't talk mainstream. Some never used a computer before they came to the school. An outline is an alien concept. As a creative writing teacher, I hear the selves kept in locked drawers. The secrets awkwardly freed, validation in 12-point font. What do they write best? The stories of their lives.

Tanika was sexually abused by her stepfather. Her mother survived a car accident, though part of her brain was scattered across the highway. Her brother, not so lucky, died in a separate head-on. She laughs when she tells me this, this cursed car-fate of those whose floorboards are rusted through. A big, glowing African American woman, her every poem is about God or friends. Generous, she doesn't know what she ought to hide, and this is her grace and protection.

Carl, quiet, gentle, and polite, communicates in painstakingly tiny penmanship; when he speaks, he is reflective. In writing he refuses to expand upon topical points, believing it's better to simply speak his mind. His encased saxophone is hauled to ear training, music theory, vocal performance, and his local quintet. Carl strode out from "the bad side" of Decatur, which is plenty rough. Layoffs have left empty homes and businesses. Decatur hasn't pulled off urban renewal, so poverty shows. The Vice Lords and Gangster Disciples stop off between Chicago and St. Louis, finding easy recruits. And Carl sits straight, talks molasses, throws around perceptive comments, and opens the door for women. The son of a minister. He greeted me with surprise. You're here?

Alicia Smote. White girl like me, pinched and cautious, black hair center-parted. Eyes like stake-holes. Child of violent divorce, a missing father, and a grandmother who languishes in drugged depression. Mom lives on the bad-track side of a small town—so small forget covering it up. Divorces there rip off the gauze too obviously; children with messy hair and hand-me-downs are patronized by teachers and the president of the PTA. Alicia's talent makes her special and weird. She plays the violin. Sings to the heavens. Grasps Jesus as concept and reality, and her every move is driven by this passionate love. Her commitment to her fundamentalist church is complete as she devotes herself to ecstasy.

Martin. Tries to hand in the same paper semester after semester, always has a reason. He plays bass guitar and saxophone, and is a baritone in an array of choirs secular and gospel. Then his mother dies and he disappears and when he comes back he doesn't fight. Just takes his F's. Martin's in the band, scrunched behind the pianist. I see the sleeve of his slick tangerine-colored shirt.

But Randy Cartier. Slight, fast, coming from two touchdowns and three interceptions, the man of the hour at every moment. When he pops into class five minutes late, it's an arm around my shoulder, it's "Hey there, Miz Bradway, how ya doin' today? What's goin' on in your *life*," never doubting that with this ridiculous charm I'll let him slide. Recruited from Chicago, he's conquering the school with looks and jokes and athletic ballet. At the basketball games he heckles the white fans from the opposing team, the TKE guys with Budweiser shirts and sports cars, hooting, egging them to even *try* calling him nigger so he can send their sorry butts to social hell. He's singing in the angel's choir on the side of the fallen ambitious ones, the ones who want more than allowed.

There are others in this band of brilliant failures whose futures are up for grabs. How can you know this story of "racial conflict-slash-harmony" if you don't know *them*? How can I show you that the ones who can't meet the medium-way expectations may finally fly over?

Once at a Lutheran sermon the soft-spoken, balding minister said that it wasn't what a person did that got them grace. You didn't have to believe, you just had to be and God would open doors. Along with fully being came a fundamental understanding of grace. Forget the charity drive, the poem of contrition, embarrassed tears. You *are* saved. The singers in the church comprehend the nature of grace. They know they are blessed and so their classes are irrelevant. The classroom is no place for joy. They're on the edges of their seats, restless to perform, full of untappable energy. They gaze out windows. Giggle and doodle. Some days I walk into a classroom and look past them, my mind heading straight outside. They know I'm fidgeting, too. Especially if it's a pretty day.

Maybe that's why I'm at this church—a Presbyterian gothic design, turn-of-the-20th-century, with wings, Gabriel in colored glass, ornate metal shades with cutout stars that let the bulbs' light through. The pews are padded and the hymnals new, with words from many cultures adapted to old English and French folk tunes. Except for today, this church nurtures the blond and brown-haired British descendants that stand politely, singing every note reverently, hiding ennui. It is designed for convocation and quiet ritual. Although there is plenty of room for dancing, such celebration would surely break the worshipful air of propriety.

The pews fill. In walks a light-skinned black woman with swept-up hair, a black tank top, and an elaborate tattoo on her shoulder. Her two small girls with red ribbons in their braids scramble into a pew, then hang over the back and watch. Beside them a couple, dressed in polyester, faces pasty as German dumplings, fidget and look down at their hands. Black women, midnight serious, cluster solemnly. The ushers, stately black men in jackets and ties, assess the crowded room, the community they know and the collegiate newcomers in jeans and baseball caps. One post-menopausal woman peacock-struts to the front in her electric blue and hat with feather, matching shoes and nude hosiery. She must be the mainstay of her congregation, probably the AME Church, never missing a service, wailing the loudest, contributing money. I've read about her in books. I feel that I am still reading this book.

A pinched and bald-headed man the color of iced tea stoops

over the lectern. He raises his hand. "Some of you think you've come to see a performance. A performance by this choir of bright young people. But you are a participant. A participant in the fields of the Lord. You will not only watch. You will not only hear. You will respond. You will act. For this is the time of action. This is the time to prove our commitment through deeds." From the audience come scattered "amens," and "I hear you, brother." "Tell us." "Praise the Lord."

"And so I want you to put your hands together and sing with us as the choir spreads upon us God's love through the music. Take part in this celebration."

The choir swings and sways down the aisle. In loud spirit they move to where a woman in a tailored azure suit waves an arm, directing them to their positions on the risers. Male singers stand in the middle, surrounded by women whose sharp bright voices drown them out. I check the program. Some who are supposed to be here aren't. People I taught last year who have disappeared into jobs, into the work of raising children. You can only hang by threads for so long. It's hard to pass your classes when every sentence sounds like street conversation, when periods and semi-colons and commas are in the places where it sounds like they should be, not where grammarians tell us they must be. Hard when you're holding down a job and taking care of babies, when childcare is more than your paycheck. When you can make more in the neighborhood than you'll ever make in an office—assuming you can get hired. Joshua, Elizabeth, Kaleka, Ann, Latasha, Michael, Corinne, Tiffany, Gloria.

The surviving members shine and ripple, a lake disturbed by natural force. They're exuberant in a way you rarely see in tired rock bands, trained opera singers, or perfectionistic jazz stylists. I freeze, feeling sadness, nostalgia, maybe regret—I can never be them. I worry whether I'm doing it right. Whether, revealing myself, people will see through my expression to hypocrisy or lack of sophistication. Logic will wind its elaborate embroidery as I examine the complications, when I could've just sung out my heart.

The songs go on forever, allowing for improvisation, loud then soft, a solo here, a voice wafting to the ceiling, like, say, Diana Ross's, like Celine Dion's, slipping into Aretha; some wail like Whitney Houston if she'd just let it out. People rise, singing back, encouraging, yelling "amen!" and "get it straight, sister," and "you got it, girl!" Fifteen minutes build into forty-five; they sway and shake and holler, and I stand with the rest, hands together in rhythm that is applause, tide against shoreline. They're hoping if they come against it enough, gently persuading, that something will rumble, break, and they will be in the kingdom. And when the song is over, we realize that it was only a song. Yet we were almost there. And the celebration begins again with the eerie riff of saxophone, the solace of keyboard, and finally the wave of voices: theirs.

Hanson and his girlfriend slip into a pew. Spiked hair, green on Mondays, blue on Tuesdays, earrings, jokes funny and stupid; a fatal trivialness. He lacks commitment. He sees it, wants it. But can't stop moving long enough to think. The girlfriend, surprisingly elegant to be with a punker, gawks. Laughs, points. "Weird," she says to Hanson, who smirks. Then he looks at the choir with such envy. Back at the girl, then drawn in again; his shoulders sway.

Tanika and four other women move from both sides of the choir, alone before us, checkers of black and red. They smile at one another for reassurance. Then Tanika's possessed soprano slices through the church. No instrumentation, no backup or support. Only testament. The showdown, confrontation, confession: open, admitting, not daring the request for redemption. In exposing the soul there is no reason to do anything else. The risk is expulsion. Rejection. What humans don't want to see, the Lord may accept. Even death row killers know this. Cast upon the waters.

Every girl has a separate statement. We don't know what burden each carries. Whether she is rebellious or obedient, outspoken or shamed into silence, a diligent student or partier, sexually open or closed, smart or silly. Maybe some have children. Are married with lovers. Are lesbians. All we know is that each is separately beautiful. Their voices stand in representation. So it doesn't matter what mistakes they've made. Who they've hurt or what they've left. Liked or despised, it makes no difference, because the voice transcends all that, unmasked alone and in harmony. The church, like the page, the stage, is the sanctuary that makes personality irrelevant. None of these women are stars; aren't famous, probably never will be, probably won't try; no billboards, promotion, arena dates; no ads, publication, notice. Just voice.

Tanika's defiant, piercing cry sails over the others'. Sondra's is a frail child's tone that stands purely alone and is lost when the others join her. A husky alto blossoms from Anita, whose long wavy hair, heavy-on-the-cream skin and high cheekbones hint at Spanish; and Shirelle slides in with the street-side near-baritone that every *a capella* on-the-corner group's gotta have. Kay's is a plain, medium talking pitch that holds the highs and lows together. They are telling it, as one woman calls out from the pews. It is hard to breathe.

When they finish in a blended crescendo, people wave hands in a gesture of faith that I don't understand. Everyone applauds, as if to keep the silence from returning, to keep the answer from coming too quickly. When we sit, I say to my husband that this kind of music comes straight from pain. This bothers him and I know it was something he didn't want to hear.

Some people's struggles are deeper. Set back from the beginning, there is more to go through. Gospel is the wrestle between slavery and freedom. The recognition that even if chains are broken, freedom is an illusion. Except in death, except in the music itself. This tension between bondage and escape, pain and release, holds a frightening sexuality. Play Aretha, James Brown, Chuck D, or even Smokey Robinson and someone will eventually protest. "You call that music?" my stepson once said. "But, but he's the *Godfather* of *Soul*," I sputtered, amazed that this wasn't enough to convince him. My mother used to turn off the TV whenever a black singer (other than Nat King Cole, who sounded like margarine) appeared on her television. "That noise," she would say, and "they sweat too much." Racism, sure. Or is it also fear of facing emotion, of what happens when we lose control, wail and cry, pace the stage, call out "Please?" Will God turn away? Will the others laugh? Will they walk to the other side of the street when they see me, pretend to misunderstand? If we reveal our pain, our secrets, will we never be able to go back to our tidy house? What if there is no tidy house? Gospel comes out of rootlessness, of being physically torn from family who are lost, sold, dead. Safety exists only in the house of the Lord (if nobody bombs it). Salvation and rebellion can be attested through reverends who advocate peaceful revolt. In the choir's call is visceral pain and demand for redemption. If the rebels seek their freedom, whose houses will burn? Will one be mine?

When the five girls take their places in the whole of the choir, the group moves into a rambunctious spiritual. Horns return to lips, voices rise in loud response. The gospel of escape. The chair, the field are temporary, the punishment passes. A soul can't be gunned down. Transcendence can't be stopped by drugs, expulsion, or bullets. In gospel music spirit is released through religion; in rhythm and blues, through sex, love, party, and fight; in art, through the act of creation and the re-creation of the act through experiencing it as a witness.

Many soul singers and rockers have spent their lives waffling between sinner and saint. Al Green is now a minister and sings only religious music. Little Richard, too. Aretha, Elvis Presley, Johnny Cash, even Jerry Lee Lewis, raised in the church, chime back to it again and again. It is a peculiarly southern understanding of poverty, oppression, despair, and, finally, release. This choir of students celebrates in a city torn by racial division, where the Klan and neo-Nazis slide pamphlets under doors, where Jesse Jackson delivered a speech only a few days before backed by this same choir.

There are so few white people in this church. Few teachers, though this is a group of student performers funded through the university; not even now during the height of racial anxiety in Decatur, when the international press is interviewing Jesse Jackson and the local white supremacist leader debates the Rainbow Coalition's lawyer on Court TV. We're so accustomed to division. Jesse Jackson will leave town and everything will be quiet. That's what they say.

The choir's voice raises the beams. Clapping, hands waving, shouting, we who once listened become the choir. Faced with this surge of joy, we must respond. I dance in my own white way, moved to a peculiar, tight heartache and a happiness that's bittersweet at best. Can it be better? . . . probably not . . . maybe. The peacock lady sings and shouts, moves in the aisle with others, filling this stately and proper high-beamed church with fundamental delight. All foes are pushed to the wall, for the only way to silence force is to barrage it—with wisdom, music, screams, or weapons. Every singer in this church knows this to the bone. Truth is a long, hard, no-speed-limit highway, traveled hands-together—and this makes it worth it, at least halfway. . . . Voice shakes the colored glass as we finally wake up.

here and now in *soy city*

back
to normal

BLADING B/N

I ROLLER BLADE. Me, forty years old, a mom, balanced on eight expensive wheels. In Bloomington/Normal, my temporary city, the Constitution Trail was provided in one fine moment of inspired civic-mindedness. The blacktopped path slices B/N in a choppy zig-zag-zig, a careful demarcation of the "good" side of town. Rarely on this trail will you find broken glass, stray rocks, or scary people—and certainly never litter. I hightail beneath

low-hanging leaves, between wildflowers and prairie grasses that remind me of home. In this town of colleges and insurance companies, the trail provides refuge from paperwork mountains.

To get access, I park in downtown Normal in the lot next to Tandemonium, an ice cream shop. It's eight-thirty in the morning, and the area is deserted. Students rarely get up this early. Pulling off my Reeboks, I stick my feet out the car door, yank green hulking monstrosities over my socks, press down three plastic clamps that keep the roller blades secure. The safety of hook in groove is nothing like the dangerous-but-fun metal key skates that pulled off my shoes as a nine-year-old. This movement is for grown-ups, my reward for having survived this long—and now I get to relive pushing up and sailing down hills, turning a perfect circle without falling.

I'm respectably good at blading, and feel embarrassed but mostly proud as I skate up the ramp of parking lot pavement to the sidewalk. In my cap, and being small, I can camouflage myself into looking not quite out of the element of youth. In Bloomington/Normal, looks count. It's not like, say, Chicago, where on a trip up to see the Cubs I saw swarms of middle-agers roller blading along Lake Michigan. In the city, independent spirits blend—there's always someone on the street way more eccentric than us. But in B/N, we don't see street people, or even untidy students (unless it's three in the morning after a frat party, and even then the hair seems stylistically messy). It's a breath-held-and-tummy-tucked kinda place; or, as I told a friend, "everyone walks around like they've got big rods up their butts." I've been here long enough—three years—that my own posture's greatly improved, and my rural/post-hippie background looks quaint. They call it assimilation.

Except on the trail. Then I feel momentarily defiant. I also feel strong, as if I own my body. This isn't a feeling I've had much. Allergic to dust, dogs, pollen, and just about everything else, and not team-sport inclined, my body's been more a hindrance to flight than a vehicle, its troublesome illnesses and desires causing me more problems than I could control. My body has caused time to slip away in wads of kleenexes and bottles of muscle relaxants. Roller blading, body and mind are in a sync nearly as absolute as passion. We move together and it's only good; no one else can be hurt if I fall—but I won't—and a physical fall is nothing like an emotional one, and at the end I won't be exhausted. I will be stronger: an inevitably positive outcome. I'm amazed at the simplicity, and this equation pushes me along the trail to the crossing at College Street.

Zipping through a break in traffic and past the bank, I slide by a girl with a backpack who is probably on her way to the university. This part of the trail cuts through a downtown of bars, coffeehouses and lunch spots, then heads west past banks and apartment houses. The lot where I parked fronts a building with windows painted on its outside white walls. A few weeks ago, my daughter watched the painter as he added puffy white clouds to an indigo sky. "Looks real good," she complimented him. "I like it. But where's the bird?" That day we stopped at

back to normal

Earthkeepers and peered at globes, stuffed giraffes, and eagles balancing on the ends of pencils, went to Babbitt's, which is floor-to-ceiling crammed full of used books I can't afford, then got a sandwich at Subway where the students hang out. Going past the raucous frat bars (German beer garden!) and the one punk bar (coming soon: Death's Head, a Marxist trio), and staring through the window of the Music Shoppe at the pianos we can't buy because we can't fit a chair into our tiny house, let alone something beautiful (though we do have a Yamaha keyboard that plays a hundred instruments), Paige and I had a good shopping day, even if we didn't buy a thing.

This will be my last year in Normal, if I don't get married. I brood about possible endings as I coast to a stop at the next block, hoping the Lexus turning the corner won't floor it and squash me. Three years ago I dropped into the false community of grad student life—identity on hold, me a place-marker—time and position marked by hoops: classes, proposal, internship, comps, proposal, dissertation. Like breezing across this street, trying to get to the other side, hoping no potholes will appear or that the pressure won't suck me down some hill or that the fun won't let me drift on a plane of nonachievement. Some people hang around the university and never finish their degrees, becoming chubbier and more uncertain as whatever status they might have had fritters away in the dawning of their defeat. A person has to push on and fast, so that ground isn't lost. If malicious gossip is tossed your way, you get through it, head ducked, eyes on the prize. (And there's so much talk! someone sleeping with someone else, students taken advantage of, teachers playing macho, cheating, scamming, bullshitting, sucking up, random pregnancies, love that's always half-assed because it's not a place made for staying.) I left a marriage and a job and started something new. So much happened and nothing happened; so much upheaval to end up back where I began, writing and researching.

BLADING B/N

Now I'm not on the government's payroll like I was at my old job, but the aristocracy's. The people who understand what I say are only the people in the academic club. Wherever I go, the club will follow and I will stay in the club. The school where I get a job will be in some ways like Illinois State, which in some ways is like the school I attended thirteen years ago. Like IBM, a network of offices and the secret handshake of those in the know. The bars on North Street and Beaufort won't be much different from the ones on the College Avenue of my future; and moving along and finding a position in life really isn't so different from collecting the three matching cards and buying a plastic green house.

Being a homebody who spent most of my life in the center of Illinois, I find this kind of interchangeable existence hard to accept. I much prefer believing that every place is distinctive and unusual, that the world is not a construction of Circuit Cities and Applebees. I glide past apartments owned by SAMI with its redbird logo; hulking buildings where the rooms look the same and students hand over their student loans to absentee landlords. B/N sucks and oozes conventional money, money invested in certificates of deposit and stock and property. The security and pomposity of cash make me want to leave, while there are people who make me want to stay. But those who love me keep at a careful distance, since B/N isn't a place for random joy or spontaneous affection. The decision of whether I remain is made in such cautious measure by almost-fiancé and me that I want to go fast and never stop. If staying has to be thought through for so long—so laden with doubts—then it must not be right. This is what I tell myself, while my heart says stay and my feet go nowhere but this trail. And I don't get reckless. I move forward carefully because there are old people walking up ahead who could get hurt.

I'm stopped. A van crawls past, displaying its "I LOVE JESUS" and Promise Keeper bumper stickers. B/N has more churches per capita, I've read, than any other city in the U.S.

back to normal

Teenagers avoid Halloween dances because this holiday is sacrilegious. My daughter's school bans fantasy books from the library because such books advocate witchcraft. I feel conspicuously heathenish.

I never drive on this side of this city. What I know of B/N is the territory of the schools, the shopping malls, and the neighborhoods between. The northwest side is full of tossed-up houses in rows and cul-de-sacs, erected so quickly I can't get over the sense that something's conquered. The landscape around B/N, its fields and woods, looks dusty and dry even after a rain, so I can't say that the beautiful is being taken. This civilization is so well-plotted—so, well, civil—that I stay in the older parts of the city, among the declining houses, each distinct in brick, stone, siding, stories, porches—garage-less—so when I'm faced with rows of matching modern homes, I don't know where I am. The only landmark is this single strip of wildness.

I glide between the stopping posts of the trail, careful not to catch a wheel on the uplifted pavement between street and blacktop. I'm far enough past the center of town that the cement stretches ahead, broken only by a pair of joggers and a woman pulling kids in a red wagon. Nobody's coming toward me, leaving it clear to build up speed and pass. When I was a walker, road-bound, it annoyed me when cyclists buzzed by, jeopardizing my safety. Now I think of pedestrians as slowpokes who'd do better to stay on the sidewalk, and I hope I never again have to see the world at such a snail's pace and without a thudding heart.

It's about being a little bit bad. Fast cars, fast guys, and the belief that something in defiance allows flight. Behind the trees are subdivision houses, yards full of play equipment and decks. My first husband and I constructed a huge wooden swing set when my daughter turned two. Built to last. I want to live again in a big, pretty house, but not one as precise and trimmed as these. I need weeds. Some sense that from chaos springs the unexpected, finding a sudden spray of sunflowers along the path—like the ones I too quickly pass. There's no time to stop. My right blade slides on squished elderberries and I nearly sway into the path of the bicyclist racing toward me at fifty mph in his Robocop helmet and glasses. The divorce came on as fast as this guy on his machine, put in the works by fear and need and talk, and I lost my comfortable backyard—at least that one, and that swing. Along with risk-taking comes the horrible awareness that it will all disappear. And maybe that's what the trimmed grass and painted houses fight against; the bushes are barricades, the lawns moats to keep away intruding people and thoughts. In B/N live men who are Promise Keepers, that right-wing religious group that tries hard to keep the nucleus from exploding. Sixty percent of the men in Promise Keepers are paying their dues for sexual sins. I read that in the local newspaper, *The Pantagraph.* Fighting temptations. The Promise Keeping men don't dare let in the idea that their women are fighting temptation, too. Instead, they buy a bigger riding mower and a rechargeable weed whacker.

Another bicyclist whips past and I don't fall. Since I'm too stubborn to wear a helmet or knee pads, a fall would be messy. I would be nearly as banged up as when I left Tim, the ex. The disaster didn't come from anything bearing down on me; it came from having a baby and being responsible not only for my future, but also for hers. The rightness of leaving made it no easier. Having been with this man for all of my adult life, the prospect of being alone was scary. Could I balance? When I fell, would the bones mend? What if I smacked into a tree and ended up the twisted wreckage from a drivers' ed filmstrip?

A muscular woman in pink shorts and a string-legged man in a gray t-shirt jog past. They huff for breath and I'm glad I'm not working that hard. Their exercise is diligent, their reward an endorphin kick. It's like office work, the tedium of driving forward. These joggers look well-kempt, well-maintained, and well-fed—nothing like the athletic frat boys or sorority sisters;

they're my age—their breathing, like mine, rasps. We need to get it done. To promote our way to self-esteem, hold our loved ones in a world where everyone scatters like seeds. To do this, we build ourselves into pillars of strength; we move forward quickly and never look back long enough to become pillars of salt. Why think of the wrecked dreams of family life when there's so much to accomplish?

I lean back on my heel, slowing for the next stopping point. The blades scrape as I approach an open soccer field. B/N not only has churches; it has parks. People donate land and pay taxes to maintain them for the public good. The city has a feeling of grand benevolence, of gifts passed to us, the children, from those whose striving made a profit. My daughter plays soccer. We need the random fields in our cities. But, coming from the country, I know this isn't really a field. A field is something entirely bigger, carrying in its furrows the expectancies and failures of livelihoods, the danger of weather.

Electric charges run up and down my right leg—I take a break, leaning against the stopping post. I have to be careful not to push so hard that I knock myself on my back for a few weeks of malfeasant nerves. It's really not good that I go for the full forty-five minutes of rush; it would be healthier to turn around and head back. But discovery is at the end, where few people go.

The soccer field may be on land once owned by the Old Soldiers' and Sailors' Home, an empty haunted orphanage now occupied by therapists' offices, homeowners, and children. I've been there a few times: once visiting a professor, another watching my near-fiancé's kid playing baseball. Maybe I'm on the fringes of its acreage. I have no sense of direction. I do know that my grandmother lived in an orphanage. It may have been this one beyond the soccer field. It had the same clean isolation, a brick institutional building like a schoolhouse but bigger, with no paper cutouts on the windows. The windows of some of the orphanage buildings are shattered, leaving jagged holes and weapon-like shards. The land is now used by teams: kids need the place. A crisis center for abused children may even take over one of the crumbling dormitories. A skating rink now stands where the tennis court used to be. Did orphans play tennis? I hear voices in the field and think of my grandma, who still won't drive a car and has always been afraid of random strangers who might approach my childhood homestead asking directions. (Grandma and Grandpa lived behind us.) She rarely speaks, and spends her days tending flowers and watching TV game shows. She especially liked Bill Cullen, but now that he's dead *Wheel of Fortune* is okay. She longs for nothing because solitude is all she's ever wanted. I cross the street.

Maybe I'm no different, traveling so far out on the trail that no one follows or approaches. I pass a desolate stretch of field and move beyond B/N's suburban order to the White Pines Trailer Court. I find the sad randomness of trailer living: cheerful chimes, a vegetable garden in a square fence, Sesame Street curtains in a child's window. Not a soul outside, but signs of life: watering cans, Big Wheels, even decks.

Whenever I see a trailer, I want to go in and curl up on a plaid couch covered with dog hair, like when I was a kid and Grandma, Mom, and I would go visit Aunt Billie in her Airstream on Clear Lake. Which wasn't a lake, but the name of one of the most dismal streets in Springfield, running in front of a Kmart, a steak house, a string of motels, and, finally, the Hay Home projects. Any trip into Springfield from the country was a treat, but Billie's trailer was an adventure. It wasn't a house, but a livable can. Aunt Billie wasn't an aunt. She was Grandma's stepmom, about the same age as Grandma. (Grandma's dad—the one who put her in the orphanage—had a string of wives. Four, I think. Billie was the last.)

Billie's trailer was small, silver, with rounded ends, and she lived in a cramped lot with other old folks. Gray-haired men cross-legged in lawn chairs, white-haired ladies walking peke-apoos. That trailer park had no grass or flowers like this slightly more upscale and near-rural B/N park does. Billie's yard was cluttered with whirling plastic daisies and praying Madonnas and carved ducks on poles. At ten, I thought it a toyland for grown-ups who weren't ready to live in real houses. I didn't realize it was all about fixed incomes and dead friends and rough living. I thought Billie liked playing cards on her gray linoleum table and crocheting Barbie toilet paper covers. And maybe she did.

I wonder if the folks in these trailers are there by choice. Or is it disability? Alcohol? What do they think when they look at the gabled houses of the B/N execs? Well, probably they think what I think—that it's unattainable, a life beyond understanding. Ties and jackets and hosiery. A mystery I only tried to enter in the past few years. My dad wore a brown uniform and carried a lunch box. He didn't own ties. When there was a funeral, he wore a suit that rode too high on his ankles. I never wanted those houses, though. Even now, when I drive by them, I shiver.

So when I push on, I do it hard. Taking big strides, picking up speed. No one is there to stop me, and it's a long way until the next road. I'm angry. Angry that . . . what? That people live in trailers? That I thought trailers were okay? That other people look down on people in trailers? Pissed pissed pissed off and I gain a wonderful speed. Every step is sure. Every step has purpose and will get me where I need to go. This is the right response. So it doesn't turn back in on me, shove me down into the pan and simmer, pushing shut the lid. The anger is out. Directed. Like gas in a line, this fuel that sparks my movement. Not righteous anger—this isn't self-righteousness; it's just mad. At the wooden bird hanging from the hook on a metal door. At how we try to make it nice when it's not nice. I'm mad that they don't burn the trailer park down. But then what would they have?

Swaying the way the teenagers sway, my body follows my direction and directs me in return. There are thickets, and I pass beneath a highway bridge and out of town. There are no places to rest. I don't want to rest.

My breath is deep but even. My body glides into autopilot. It's clear and I'm where I need to be. Moving. Not working, not concentrating, but flying. Flight under control.

I need to cross. My friend Sharmina and I used to zoom our bikes down a backwoods road that ended at a wooden bridge. Racing down the hill so fast our feet couldn't stay on the pedals, hitting the bridge with a lift, sailing until we bumped against the slats. The boards provided a hilarious shake-up that dissolved our breaths into huh-huh-huhs and our stomachs jarred and we never puked. We never thought to be afraid. Up the slope of the arched bridge, then down, a pothole waiting at the end where the blacktop met us—whack. This could throw a wheel. Just as, pushing faster and faster, if I hit slick pavement, or a stick, I could skid and knock my back out of line, walk around like a hunchback for weeks. Except I won't fall.

At school, I've passed my comprehensive exams, those days of testing that allow us to graduate. Now it's the clear sailing of dissertation. Pushing, pushing; otherwise, I might curl like fern fronds and caterpillars, rolling into a ball. Energy builds until I can do no less than go.

On the slope, I catch my breath. I'm luckier and lazier than the joggers who thud, thud, thud without respite. I coast until I come to the final crossing: Raab Road.

The cars and trucks leave town, picking up speed to travel the country. I lean against a post, waiting for traffic to pass, imagining that the drivers notice I'm not a young ponytailed chick. Across the road, a dump truck makes a U to one of the heaps of sand piled like mini-pyramids. These humps of dirt rise on either side of the trail; beyond is a grain elevator on the right, and to the left, an industrious-looking building set back by the highway. At the edges, the trail is accident: brush, scrub trees, flowers.

back to normal

Cars brake and I zip onto the last mile of the trail. Wind hits hard without the windbreak on the right, and sand stings my face. This is the country—I recognize it. Nothing to stop what nature's out to give you. It's not only the absence of people, because other parts of the trail are free of subdivision clutter. It's absence of plan—angular plots and well-placed foliage—and presence of gust. I take in delicate blue blooms, baby's breath, random white daisies. Weeds, too, because who cares? The man driving the dump truck? The man minding the cash register at the feed store down the way? The man working the grain eleva-tor?—Men, because, it being the country, these jobs won't be filled by women. Affirmative action, gender equity are city terms for sophisticated problems that country people pretend they don't have. We settle our problems one-on-one. Women work only if they have to, and with this comes shame. Nothing is a matter of decision. Everything is random, like the cloud that comes out of nowhere and hangs above my head, darkening the path. I'm glad for it—I'm sweaty and hot, though it's a perfect eighty. In the country, we let things be, which means not a lot happens that doesn't happen *to* us; when we do things, we pre-tend we didn't. So I blade past the elevator where someone left a rusting green tractor and implements meant to rake and sow the fields; maybe they've been there for years, the owner dead or otherwise departed. Or maybe whoever owns the elevator thinks it's art, beautiful in its starkness beside the weathered white silo. But I doubt it.

Finally, I stop. Homesick for space; amazed at silence. The only sound is the motor of the single truck. There are days when it's not even that. The elevator is never operating when I come by; I don't know if it's my early morning hours, or if it has been abandoned like the tractor. Something is lost and captured about the Farm Supply Store, its single room, its one window; like the store destroyed in the town where my cousins were raised, it's past its time. Beyond the store are fields of soybeans, reminding

BLADING B/N

65

me of Midwestern purpose. Except farmers don't gather around the stores, which have long since been sold to outside businesses that hire workers to run them. Just as workers don't hang out in small-town grocery stores to carry on generations-old gossip. The generations have died away or are moving on or are planning to move on. Maybe a student works at the Farm Supply Store now, instead of Buddy Clayhorn's son (or Betty's boy, or Sam's cousin).

The isolation of the country has always carried mourning. Predicting its own demise, and mine. When I come out here, my eyes water. I tell myself it's the wind, and not something I've lost and given away so that I can wear makeup and skirts and grade papers and think abstract things that would make my uncle, the carpenter, laugh. If no one is at this grain elevator, maybe it's because there's nothing left to give the restless sons and daughters who, like me, moved away. This is change, brought by the magic of TV that gave us the big world and made us realize that this quiet, slow land was empty. We lost our will to defend it. No one wants it. The majesty of this silo is that of a dying civilization. It's beautiful because no one cares, its purpose is stripped, it is a barren isolate. Like me, who chooses to be on the far end of the trail on a sweet summer day, who relishes not being seen and is thrilled when the truck drives away, who can imagine a life entirely alone. I have lost my immediate purpose, as I blade to the wildflowers. Pink ones cringe in the underbrush, wrapped by a vine. I could pick them, but they would wilt before I got them in a vase. Their purpose is to be here. To inhale and exhale.

I push on. Across the road, I'll get back among the houses. I can get home and shower, put on body lotion and perfume, powder and mascara that will make me look less an aging free spirit and more a professional, and when I find flowers, I'll buy them at Jewel/Osco for $3.50 if there's a sale. I'll grade papers so the students will know where they stand. There will be no dirty knees—not even on my daughter—and certainly no crocheted

back to normal

covers for my toilet paper. Instead, my wall has a reproduced Klee.

When things are clean and in order, we're not as likely to get sick. To lose track, become swamped or confused. When I was a kid, I loved the small dark rooms of the subdivision houses where my friends lived—houses that didn't ramble into added rooms, where the living room wasn't in the basement, like mine. Those lives were compact. The bedrooms cheerful, with shelves and well-made beds with real comforters. Basements with ping pong tables and dart boards. They knew their manners in an offhand, subconscious way that I still don't.

Now I can turn awkwardness into a sort of charm by being funny. If people laugh, I could care less. I'm in between—not wilderness, not high rise.

The wind in B/N proper never whips through as sharply as it does here, across open, flat land. When I turn around and head back, the wind keeps pushing, and I fight it until the trees and fences provide protection and I can just coast.

THE BETTER PORCH

WE SIT ON THE NEWLY BUILT front porch of one of the houses on my street—a street of squat, sided homes for people a step up from trailer living, a block from the motorcycle dealership, the pawnshop, and Mission Mart. The porch winds around the front and sides of Abigail's house and has cutouts of hearts and flowers: Abby's own design.

She and her husband Scooter have been putting the porch together piece by piece, because they can't afford to hire a carpenter. Late into the night, the whine of saws and the thump of nails keep the neighborhood awake. Sometimes comes music, the Smashing Pumpkins singing "1979" or their daughters' electric guitars screaming through open bedroom windows. When I moved to South Hill (the name of our little neighborhood, as in "Why would you live in South Hill?") I saw the blond one juggling in the street, her brother roller blading circles around her in his Pearl Jam t-shirt. Outlaws on this road where everyone else tries so hard to be respectable by hiding their alcoholism (Roger and Courtney next door), thievery (Bettie, arrested for skimming from the donut shop where she worked for ten years), weirdness (Bobby, a ten-year-old on the corner who takes polaroid snapshots of other boys' butts).

I stick my feet up on Abigail's unpainted railing and drink a beer. Beside me is Joe, who brought bratwursts from his night job bartending at Pub I. During the day, he drives a school bus and works part-time at Mitsubishi while he waits to get on "the list" that will give him a union wage and benefits. "Aren't they great?" Joe says, when I bite into my dog and bun. "Didn't I tell you?" Joe is balding and wears aviator-frame glasses. He might be anywhere from twenty-five to forty, thin and pale and buffeted by so many storms that he's always blinking. His two sons sit on the porch behind us, squirming like octopuses as they eat from flimsy paper plates. His wife left him for a trucker, who left her for a waitress—and now she's moved back in, according to Abby. "Poor Joe," is Abby's refrain. "Such a nice guy to be married to a bitch. She can't be a woman, the way she abandons those kids." The five-year-old clings onto anyone, me included, like fluff on a sweater. He does this now, tugging at my waist, leaving ketchup finger marks on my second-hand designer shirt. He's light as the spine of a feather. Not substantial like Paige, my daughter, who fights with Abby's son Clay over a chip that's dropped on the wooden planks.

"Your daughter likes Clay now. Last week it was Ryan. She plays my sons for fools. And they love it. Why is it that they're happiest when you're toying with them?" Abby puts a hand on a big hip draped with flimsy tie-dye. Her teenaged daughters, progeny of the marriage with the rich lawyer, tell her she ought to dress like Mama Cass and come with them up to Chicago when they party with the Smashing Pumpkins. Nia, the youngest, is dating one of the Pumpkins, though she hasn't yet turned eighteen. There was a picture in *Rolling Stone,* Nia moving down a sidewalk like a runway model, arm in arm with this musician who appears to be a china doll. Nia has decided not to go on to college, though she was offered a scholarship at the Art Institute. Instead, she'll go into PR.

"He wants to marry her," Abby tells me. "I used to look like her. I used to be that thin—Hey, Scooter! Didn't I used to look like an actress? I looked like, who's that girl on *Friends*?"

"I dunno," I say. I never have time to watch TV; between my daughter, my fiancé, and grad school, time spirals away like graffiti down a toilet.

"Uh-huh." Scooter exchanges a look with Joe before flipping a burger on the grill. They both snicker.

Nia gets out of the purple car shared by her and her sister, walks up the dirt yard carrying a sack. (The yard is dirt because, while the hearts are carved in the porch railing, the sod hasn't yet been laid, or the roof redone, or the siding put on the front of the house.) Nia moves like a specter in ballet slippers; her hair is white and clipped like a smooth flapper's hat, her shirt over white shorts is a shade of lime green never found in limes. Her brows are arched lines like those of a friend of my mom's thirty years ago, her lips a bauble of pink. "School bores her," Abby says as Nia coasts up the steps. "Bored me, too. That's why I'm here with a master's degree and four kids. The administration kept telling me how to teach." Abby puts out an arm as Nia starts to pass. "Whatcha got for us?" she says, peering into the sack.

"Shoes," says Nia.

"Why don't you try them on and show us?"

"No thanks, Ma." She keeps going, the door slapping shut behind her. A mottled cat in the kitchen window looks at me. The house would seem cozy but for the boards propped beside the door, the chain saw on the ground, the sawdust. This is the second summer for renovations, the second summer I've lived here. I think they may have started the summer before.

"She's a size 5. My feet were size 5 when I was in art school. I always went barefoot. I worked with the deKoonings. They came for a semester of workshops. I was the youngest in the class; I got out of high school early and was a protégé. A protégé. Smart as Nia. Smarter than Nia. I was a latter-day hippie, but I had to give all that up."

Husband. Children. I know the arc of this story. When I was young, I used to think it was an excuse. My friend Daisy, never sending out her writing, never following her dream of schmoozing Toni Morrison in New York. How can I? she'd said. I have the kids. Megan, wife of a published novelist, novelist herself, the novel never revised, never mailed, still living its lovely fantasy in a file drawer: three kids and a job as a reporter. And what happened next? When Daisy's children grew, she was tired from working as a saleswoman to pay her debts, and wrote only chatty essays for the newspaper, and Megan devoted herself to a million causes and no longer needed to free those characters. The characters died. Well, Daisy died of cancer. And me? I have a daughter and no husband, am trying to take my comps and have monumental debt, but characters still come knocking, making their demands, and I can't turn them away. I'm irresponsible. This is what I think as I look through the heart-shaped hole cut into this wooden railing. I live in a rental house. I'm "on the verge" of being engaged, which means I probably will be but might not be, to a divorced professor who lives in a rambling ranch house. I have to write my dissertation and find a job, which may mean actually getting a job but might not. I have a mound of school loans and a kid who needs a suit for the swim team. I don't know where I will live next year.

"I didn't used to live this life. I had a house by the lake," says Abby. "A beautiful home in the country. Brick. A screened-in porch. Five acres and from the living room, our bay windows, you could see the duck pond. I taught art at Knox College."

Maybe we aren't listening. We know this story already. Scooter sits on the raised steps, his feet on the dirt where more bricks will go. His dirty finger follows the carved imprint in a brick. 1910. He looks like a grown-up little boy, the way his blond hair enfolds his face like a bowl. He looks like his sons.

"He gave me everything," Abby says. "And what's the view here? The Pilgrim Heritage Church." She waves her arm at the spare white house down the street with its hand-lettered sign and nothing even close to stained glass. The minister's wife stands atop the church steps while her two daughters run along the sidewalk. All of them, even the wife, wear their long brown hair in two neat braids without ribbons.

"They're friendly enough," says Joe. "The minister and his friend, they come help me move my branches when I trimmed the tree. So I helped them dig up that back lot for parking."

"They ain't bad people," Scooter agrees. "Just got a little too much religion." The minister's wife looks over at us, then down into her tiny black purse, as if she's searching for money or Kleenex. Then she closes it. I imagine I hear its snap, like my mom's purses I played with as a kid with the big '50s clasps. And she stands with her gloved hands folded over the strap.

back to normal

"Her ears are burning." Joe wipes ketchup off his face with the back of his hand.

"They're a bunch of wacko fanatics. A cult!" Abby laughs. "Wouldn't be surprised if they're in there praying to E.T.— Ryan! Pick that bun up! Do you think I made this porch for you to get mustard all over it?" She walks over and whacks him on the side of the head.

"Yeah, you want mustard on it," mutters Ryan, but picks up the bun. He sticks it on my daughter's plate to get a rise out of her. Paige slugs him.

"The church is alright," I say. On Wednesday evenings, I look through the windows of my house and watch the worshipers go in and out. I'm always surprised by how loud they are, how their arguments carry down the block, and by the sad awkwardness of their children when they play games in the vacant lot beside my house. In their white shirts, stiff dresses, they jut out the plastic bat, swing madly at the whiffle ball like swatting at gnats. A friend who's into true life murders told me that David Hendricks, off the hook for allegedly killing his family, had gone to that same church. I want to take the pious little girls into my house and cut their hair, let them wear jeans, and play Beck and Al Green so that they might learn rhythm. Are they allowed to dance? The girls in front of the church whirl like tops until they fall into piles of skirt on the sidewalk.

"Look at that house across the street," Abby says. "What an ugly porch. They want a porch like mine. They want one an artist built, because they know I designed this. They used to live in a trailer court. They never went to school. My mother still calls and asks why I live this white trash life. Why are you with that man who works at Mitsubishi? Why don't you teach at the university? It's so's I can raise my kids. And my husband is a good man. So what, he's not educated."

I catch a look at Scooter. But Scooter never speaks. He stares into the flames on the grill.

"We're better than the trash across the street," she says.

THE BETTER PORCH

"There's not even any comparison."

"My house is junky," I venture. "I don't own it."

"But you're going places." Abby gets this glassy look in her green eyes. She squints at me, like she can't see well out of her bifocals. "When you get out of school, you and Paige can buy a house. Maybe that one. Maybe down the next block."

But I won't stay here. I'll marry and move to the good part of town. Into Normal, the decent section of this doubled city, leaving behind Bloomington, rent, broken toys, and the way I grew up. At my fiancé's, the beer's in bottles. The bratwurst isn't stolen.

The kids run off the porch like a pack of dogs, thumpthumpthump in big tennis shoes, to the vacant lot. "I'm it!" one yells. "You're it!" In the neighborhood where my fiancé owns his house, they don't play tag. Or red rover or hide-and-seek. The neighbors are old. The yards don't go far enough. Flowers might be disturbed.

"What's the matter, Paige?" I hear one of the boys yell. "Don't you want to get dirty?"

"Thing is," Abby goes on, "my ex, Mister Lawyer, Mister Money-and-Good-Life, he beat the crap out of me. Shoved my head through a window. I ran in my daughter's room to get away. Never figured he'd follow me in there. But he did. He shoved my head through the window. See?" She lifts her brown bangs. There it is, a scar like a white thread lacing her forehead. "If the blinds hadn't been shut, he would've decapitated me."

I'm not sure I see the logistics of this, but I believe it. "A violent man," Abby says, nodding calmly, like making an observation about soup—Oh, it's hot, it's got noodles. "An evil man. I was okay before that. He tried to keep the money. But I got support. Took him to court. Threatened to kill me. Said I was bad for the kids—in court, he says this. Not a good man. Not like Scooter here."

Scooter nods: he's heard it all. His eyes have deep bags, the only things that make him look his age. He looks at Joe. Maybe he'd like to kill her sometimes, too. That's the look. It's a joke. Joe laughs and sticks his feet up on the railing.

"You won't be allowed to stick your dirty feet up there once I get this thing painted." Abby swats at Joe.

"I guess I need more to do," she goes on. "Once I finish this work. I could go back and teach. Like you. I was a good teacher. I got ideas. I'm innovative. I challenge kids. But this house takes up all my time. And Scooter, working three jobs. What a hard-working man. Taking care of his kids. My mom doesn't understand. So we don't have money. So what."

At the end of the block, the grown son of the Vietnam vet who owns the motorcycle shop revs his Harley. Vroooom, a rage of testosterone. The son lived next door to me before he got kicked out for not paying his rent. He used to stand in his yard, looking toward my living room window.

He tears down the street. One of the kids jumps back from the curb.

"Charlie," says Abby, shaking her fist at the motorcyclist. "His dad needs to put him on a leash."

"Charlie's gonna get himself killed," says Joe.

"I'm going to do it if he hits one of the kids," says Scooter. Though he doesn't look like he could kill bugs.

"Who needs money?" says Joe. "We have bratwurst."

"Working people share." Abby leans against the post, arms crossed, glasses sliding a little down her nose. Flecks of green paint dot her arms. "That's why I watch Joe's kids for free. The kids down the street. I give up my art for kids."

And never has to leave her porch. What would it be like, to spend a lifetime on a porch? Enclosed by wood, hearts, and tulips? My grandma lived that way, in her country house with its chimes and flowers, its water pump because for awhile there was no running water. I grew up that way, enclosed by a family-built porch railing, listening to my aunt and mom and grandma gossip while they drank coffee, waiting for the men to pull up in their pickup trucks. Then the women would clean fish, skin the hunted animals, wrap the flesh in white freezer paper.

"So where you been keeping yourself?" Abby says. "We don't see much of you." Accusing. Abby is lonely. Starved for smart conversation.

"Well, I have to study for comps and teach and grade papers and take Paige to swimming meets and spend time with Doug, and. . . ." I trail off. They're all three looking at me enviously. Pissed. Like I'm showing off. On the way out. Working for the way out. Selling out. It's not the union label. They're working on their porch.

"You must be busy," Abby says.

"It's not that much fun," I add. "I mean, it's a lot of work. I'd rather be home, hanging out with Paige." And I mean it. But yet. Being a kid: Long summer days of soaps, *Hollywood Squares,* novels I'd read five times because there was no getting anyone to make the drive to the city library. Of watching the heat shimmer in front of my face, listening to the lawn mowers, the water in the sink, the saw like the sound of the chain saw down here at Abby's while my family put together its life, their porches, their cool places to sit. And then stopped. And looked at each other.

"I would love to stay here with you all," I say, drinking the last of my Budweiser, which has that warm aluminum can taste that reminds me of summer. I put the can to my forehead. I have no air conditioning in my little house. I'm as tired as Scooter who will be laying more brick before it gets dark. And my porch is leaning and needs swept. My fiancé's house, it doesn't have a porch; it looks directly out on a cul-de-sac. But his railing wobbles, which I find reassuring; like there will still be things for us to fix together and to build—his good Normal life, it's not so perfect. "But I have, you know, like this thing I have to write on," I say, feeling as embarrassed and ashamed as I did as a kid when I left my family there to talk because their stories started sound-

back to normal

ing so much the same, and I needed, so much needed, new ones.

"I'm sure glad I don't need to bother with that whole kiss-ass system," says Abby, brushing her hair back from her forehead as she turns away. "Hey, Scooter, looks to me like you got that brick a little crooked."

"Oh. What?" says Scooter, and he will fix it, and fix it again.

ASK LORD BYRON

I'D SEEN THE WHOLE THING in the newspaper, but I hadn't realized he was one of them. "Marty's in a lot of trouble," Jeff wrote in objective cyberspace script. "He's got a Class X and a Class 3 felony. Transporting heroin."

I'm in the typing pool. A doctoral student sits at the computer next to mine; Irene, the secretary, reads *People* at her desk. "Aw, shit!" We aren't supposed to raise our voices with obscene ejaculations in the Upright Department of Upright State University. Only thirty years ago men were advised not to wear their hats in the building and I'm treated better when I wear a dress. I read on.

"Since I work at the paper, I hear stuff," Jeff writes. "Looks like they were watching these guys and picked who they thought was important. I knew from class he had problems, but never thought it would be anything like this."

"One of my best students got busted," I say to the woman next to me, who blinks behind her pink plastic glasses. Nobody believes in tragedy. Not in the real world. We believe in rolling with the punches. People get what they deserve.

The doctoral student goes back to her paper.

I ask Jeff for more. Who's involved? Was he really dealing, or just sleeping on the floor? I don't ask if he was using; everyone in the class knew he stuck needles in his arm. He wrote fifty poems about it.

I scan past the professorial names from our department listserve (debating tenure, promoting potluck) and open my next personal message. It's from Jane.

"Guess you heard about that stupid asshole Marty," it says. "I know I shouldn't care, because he set out to destroy himself. But I keep thinking about how decent he was. I feel like somebody's died."

I close the e-mail program and go out to a hallway swarming with students. Like in a factory, everyone's clocking in and out. I've worked in three places with time clocks: the hospital, UPS, and a plastic-bag production line. At school we don't stand in rows; we just run for the exits.

I go to the office I share with three other doctoral slaves. Our door is plastered with *X-Files* clippings and rock-and-roll testaments, along with colored folders where students drop off their writing. We're across from the elevator, and if we leave the door open, people we don't know peek in. Kim, the *X-Files* freak, is trying to connect the ethernet. Our plug falls out of the wall. She's on her knees beneath the desk.

"Guess what, Kim? One of my students got hauled in on that big drug bust."

She emerges, glances at me, and starts fiddling with the computer's mouse. A big woman, she wears baggy Levis and five earrings. "Oh, yeah?" She makes a face.

"He was so talented," I say. "Such a good person."

She looks at me skeptically. *Contradiction?* Good people don't shoot heroin.

"Yeah. He was. Is. Sweet."

"Hm." Kim tests the RS6000 e-mail icon. The screen unfolds like a stop-motion flower and there's our ability to send and receive.

"Marty was a romantic. He never would've used e-mail. He wrote poems." I'm talking about him like he's dead.

Kim frowns at the list on her screen. Marty had wild slanted

back to normal

handwriting that got cramped, slid off the page, never appeared on the due date, would finally turn up two weeks later with an extra twenty anguished poems that told me about the beauty of heroin, that told me how visions were destroying him, how they'd turned ugly, how he was afraid, how he knew what was coming and how he didn't have to say that he just couldn't stop.

"His parents were detectives."

"That's interesting." From the wall Mulder and Scully join her in that blank, evaluative stare. "What kind of detectives?"

Handcuffs. Uniforms. Not kinky, the way we like to snigger at what is real oppression; more in a daily-life kind of way. Do this. Stay. Don't move. Duck. They keep order. Marty breaks order.

"I don't know what kind."

"Be funny if they were narcs."

Old portfolios of student writing rest on the office shelves. Marty's is there, mixed among the rest. A white manila accordion folder with doodles in the same green ink as his poem drafts. Clouds, birds.

"What's my responsibility here?"

"I don't see where you come in," she says.

"We all knew. He told us every chance he could."

"Sounds like he wanted you to know."

"But what do you do? The writing isn't the person. If I turned in something in workshop, I wouldn't want everyone to assume it was literally me, even if they would assume that anyway."

"Of course they would. That goes without saying."

Writing has boundaries, white margins that ought not to be crossed. The trespassing from fiction into not just fact, but souls, secret souls, is why people stop taking writing classes, stop writing. The more confessional the writing, the more necessary the space. Marty erected enormous white fences.

"Knowing doesn't mean you could've done anything."

ASK LORD BYRON

"It's not even that I have a problem with drugs—"

She looks at me like I'm nuts.

"I mean, nothing moral. Some of my best friends have been drug addicts. . . ." I dwindle off. Most of the grad students have focused their lives on school. Whereas I'm almost forty and have had an array of jobs, part-time ones I worked three or so at once, and one that I had ten years. The ten-year one in social services put me in touch with crisis. I've done things, too.

I knew guys who measured out pot on scales; traded it for cash; set up overweight girls to sell them diet pills; got cocaine in the mail. And I knew the women who stayed with these men; who used drugs to run away, to see their goddesses.

Enter a corner of that life and the room opens up with every step. Down the hallway is more. In the bathroom and on the balcony.

Walk into the wrong party. Try to get out again.

You could say they're lost souls, but it's nothing that melodramatic. You could say it's fun, but it's not that simple. There's flatness, hopelessness, and nothing else to do. Also the thrill of breaking the law.

I think Marty liked that.

An old boyfriend's brother was a penny-ante dealer back in the late '70s. I was nineteen, naïve and curious. Growing up in the sticks, spending my hours reading, I'd heard about drinking and cocaine and marijuana from friends, in whispers, but I'd never tried anything. I was embarrassed at being so sheltered; my friends took me to bars and were amused that I didn't know how to flirt or drink. Thing is, once I started drinking, I liked it. I giggled and still didn't know how to flirt, and I watched. I met Benny, a jazz musician, a composer who preceded all the current techno beats by making sampling tapes in his basement on a gigantic Teac tape machine. He was the allure and destructiveness of the mystical, the visionary, the close-to-the-edge that all artists want, crave, need, and that, when let loose and unattended, chews us up. I cast my lot with Benny.

back to normal

The '70s were post-'60s: hippies stuck in the light show or the stoned asleep on the grassy hill. Even my nicest boyfriend, another Ben, a minister's son, had a friend who did and sold quaaludes. A bearded guy who worked at the Decatur ADM factory and saw no reason to have energy, be hopeful, or give a shit. Why not quaaludes? Why not walk through water when no water exists? Everyone stared for hours at the TV—Ray Harryhausen movies, maybe the *Seven Voyages of Sinbad,* the original stop-action, living and reliving someone else's horrible childhood with an alcoholic dad and a lithium-zombied mom; other friends' parents who were alcoholics, or prescription drug–dependent; and my own parents, straightening the knick-knacks and not watching anything too hard, a sitcom laugh track. But the desire to chemically flee and mutate isn't always a gift from our parents. Some of my friends' families were quiet, normal, routine. Farmers and state workers. My first husband and our friends Ro and Annaleise and the rest ate mushrooms in front of Fellini movies. The place, the time, the people. Disorder and lethargy and being on the fringes. Desires underneath— who loved who. Who wanted. Who was lonely. Who didn't care. Under the languidness of smoke, or sharpened by the powder and the pills, angles and corners.

I saw myself as a recorder of deeds who would write what it was "really" like. I hung out with friends in friendly bars, hung out with friends in living rooms, saw things, inhaled, tasted, drank—in such small quantities that they were skeptical of me; they knew I wasn't a player. One thing we didn't do was inject. We saw that as hard-core, an addict thing. My friends never saw themselves as needy, even when they spent hundreds of dollars for pot that had to be smoked every morning. Or when they hit the scotch bottle every night. That was daily maintenance, done to get through the dead end jobs like my ex's filing records at the hospital, or Ro's checking statements for the Finance Department, or Lisa's hauling feed. Away from day jobs, my ex was a writer, Ro a photographer (who took the only decent picture of me), and Lisa a jewelry maker. Substances were part of the creative experiment.

Looking at a classroom, I guess who will chase dangerous visions and who will never try, and who approaches her illusions cautiously. Marty was easy; he wore the slacker trappings of those kids—kids, now, right? my own drug experiments being fifteen years behind me—who have nerve. Illinois State is full of education majors who aren't sure why, who view college as a stop-gap as they put off growing up, a necessary evil for a piece of paper. They might drink on the weekends, but are otherwise controlled. Raised securely, and with heads squarely on shoulders, they know their limits.

Marty's skin was darker than the shining blonds and tinted-blond Germans and English who dominate the central part of the state; his hair was black and close to his scalp like a cap. He was from Chicago, his parents were tough, he wore earrings and headphones, slouched through the hallways with a benign, beatific look, an apostle who'd made a wrong turn. Poetry, he claimed, was religion.

The university values ranking and doing what needs to be done to get to the next step. Romanticism is old-fashioned, the opposite of postmodernism, which is that fragmented yet weirdly rational way of piecing together an insane world by claiming it can't be pieced together. Romanticism is irrational belief in the individual; it's the individual rebelling against an all-consuming social force. I know: I had to look it up to write my dissertation, just when I thought romanticism had something to do with love and magic and adventure. Postmodernism says that people like Marty exist as part of the social landscape; they have a voice, but all voices are shared; poetry is not a particular art but a chip of the big mosaic, a little Wal-Mart here, a little Simpsons there, and maybe some Yeats. But people like Marty believe, really believe, that their songs must cut through, make sense, fly, beat against the door—before they come beating

back to normal

down the door for you. The edge is urgent, the moment before the door is broken through. Do you break it? Or does it break you? That's the challenge of the drug. Or the art.

Marty was in two of my classes: creative nonfiction and creative writing. If he wasn't in love with the project, his work was half-assed, though everything he wrote had style. He could've cared less whether he had anyone's sanction. His world was impression and picture. That first semester, metaphors flew. He was in touch. He met God. Along with the required essays came poems. Stylistic prose fragments swirled from the mundane (watching the detective parents, TV) to the sublime (music—he played, what else? the saxophone). All was jazz.

His work came in pieces. He couldn't pull it together. He thought what he was pumping into his veins had brought him to the heavens. He believed that music was the substance consumed. William S. Burroughs, Oscar Wilde, Ken Kesey, Courtney Love, Charlie Parker, heroin, opium, magic mushrooms. F. Scott Fitzgerald, William Faulkner, you name it, alcohol. Insight in madness. The rent in the opaque cloth of daily life. Flash of light. Swirl. Space.

What I saw when I was high terrified me, which may have been a good thing; otherwise, I might be sharing Marty's fate.

That old boyfriend, Benny the jazz musician, took speed and stayed up nights and days running, composing in his basement. Snippets of connected sound were ambient, beautiful in distortion, but amphetamines and neuroses made him so paranoid that he never performed or sent around the tapes. He was, by his own admission, a sociopath.

This is the part about being an artist that nobody likes to talk about. Talented, wounded people crawl into holes of quiet instability. Agoraphobics—or hermits, we used to be called, who get forced out only by monetary responsibilities. This artist's tendency gets set by drug use. Or drugs ease the painful sensitivity, the feeling of being out of the flow, out of time. It was in Marty's poems: staying in the house, staring at the screen, hiding under blankets. Poor Benny had a stroke, then moved to San Francisco, where he thought he could reclaim that illusory '60s freedom. Who knows if he did.

Why care about sordid situations and souls drifting in errant highs? Just say no, right? (Or, as my friend Jae's t-shirt read: Just say Moe, making me think of a couple of fingers in the eye, whoop, whoop. Jae always blamed her inability to travel out of town on acid flashbacks; acid taken back when she was in college, in Carbondale, a notoriously rowdy party town—but I don't believe in flashbacks. I think she just didn't want to go.) When I tell people about Marty, they frown, as if such things are best left unspoken, attraction to the destructive holy muse being a moral infringement. The anti-drug promotions make pariahs of screw-ups. Criminals of fools evil and divine. An act of desperation and self-immolation is punishable for more years than you'd get for killing someone. Murder is mainstream; drugs are dangerously counterculture or minority, and these are people we'd just as soon see die. When lines are crossed, daring fools must pay.

I ran into another student from that class, Jim, a PR major. Not a screwy bone in his body, because humor keeps him from teetering too far one way or the other. Jim said of Marty, "He's not like those other guys, man. He shouldn't be in jail. It's going to kill him. That guy's a poet."

Those who knew him qualify it to each other: "I know he did this stupid thing, but . . . ," or, from the fiction writers, "That's a crazy poet for you." Shaking our heads. Not finding the sense.

In class, we responded to his work as if he were discussing pie-making, or playing "Smoke on the Water," or skydiving. The word "heroin" never came up. We politely pretended that Marty wasn't writing about hallucinations and drug-induced paranoia. There was even, among some of the class, a pact that this

back to normal

visionary lyricism was pretty cool. On the edge. Like Perry Farrell of Jane's Addiction, Marty's hero. The ultimate in hip, just as it has always been for true romantics. Ask Lord Byron.

The drug, which dominated nearly every poem, was Marty's right as he proclaimed the need to be an artist in a streamlined world. Drugs became the metaphor, the cohesion, the reference point. What happened to music? Heroin ate it. In fleeing reality, reality got him. That's the twisted thing about escape. In trying to run away, we become captured by enforced ennui, by our own physical deterioration. Like a bad desk job.

I wrote it on Marty's poems. It was one of the few times I'd had the impulse to intervene. People write about rapes, attempted suicides, parents' divorces—they write about life—and I comment about how effectively they've laid it all out there, avoiding the topic except in a technical way. Although friends conjecture that Marty was giving the archetypal "cry for help," I don't believe that. Marty was an artist, following, as he saw it, a tradition. He didn't want me to say, Get thee to rehab.

But I did. In a teacherly sort of way.

He wore that smug look of people who chronically break the law. Everyone else looks silly, with their skirts and good behavior and subdivision house and extra cash. The world has a Barbie doll feel. A social game sense, and you're the one outside the stadium looking through the diamonds in the fence. To Marty, I had crossed the line and belonged with the straight world. I guess he was right. I would never again find myself in the International House of Pancakes in the early morning with two long-haired musicians who'd been up all night playing drums and upright bass while I wrote poems. Everyone in the pancake house staring because we were so obviously not the types with the little kids ducking under the booths. Now I have a kid. And when I see young people who've been up all night, I worry about them, though I know they're forging their own choices. Would I trade being up all night for the earthquake that followed, when I fell through the chasms as if I were another tricked Wile E. Coyote? There isn't a choice. Devils and angels come out at night.

Once he showed up at my office. He sat in the chair catercornered to my desk. Pushed up against the wall, between the filing cabinet and me. He had on his baggy everything, silver hoop earrings, and a Walkman hanging like a talisman around his neck. He's not much taller than I am, with dark and slanted eyes, and a general air of thinness. His skin is olive-colored, but he still manages to be pale.

He knew he had a gift. I didn't need to tell him that. "I'm tired of baseball," he started out. "But I'm here on scholarship. I used to think baseball was what mattered. I've done it so much, now it's only work. But if I quit, I'm out of school."

"You should throw yourself into poetry."

"I want to, man. But I can't see where to go with it. What kind of life could I have? It's not like people pay you to write poems."

"You could be a college teacher," I suggest.

"Do I look like a teacher?"

"Maybe. Why not?"

He shrugs. "Nobody in my family went to college. It seems weird."

"Well, it is, sort of. But it still beats working at a factory."

He shakes his head. "Journalism. I thought that might be okay. But writing that way. All that order. It's not me."

"Poetry has order, too. But, yeah, you make your own choices," I say. "You have to believe in it." *Come on, Marty,* runs through my head.

"What if I'm not good enough?"

"You'll get good. You just need to practice. Like music."

His voice gets quiet. "Well, are there, like . . . any classes I could take? I was looking at the guide, but I didn't know who'd be good to work with."

back to normal

I give him names. I think of my own long haul and wonder why I should be sending him on this moon-driven path. What if he tries and is slaughtered in workshop? What if he can't bring the visions together? In my writing class, he wouldn't critique other people's poetry. "Poetry, it's like love, man," he said. "You can't think about it like that." And I agree, while I know he will have to, if he's to make his love his job. It's survival, getting to earth, but we need the flight too or it won't take off. *Balance,* I thought, feeling too old even to be talking to him.

"Just get in a poetry class," I say, hoping it will be okay.

Why didn't he do it? Maybe he still thought he was a journalist, or the next Ryne Sandburg. Maybe he thought he needed a good job. Or lacked commitment. Or thought being a real artist would drive him mad. Or just didn't get around to it. I never figured Marty would end up in jail.

After the bust he tells me that it's the way people look at him that he can't stand. It's one of the last warm days. Leaves are changing yellow and red, yet only a few fall on the mazed sidewalks. On the quad Marty and I chat, catching snide looks, since his face was all over TV; down the sidewalk stands a man in a suit and sunglasses who looks like an undercover cop off of, say, *NYPD Blue.* Marty's out on bond. Taking classes; trying to keep normal, he says.

He's lost his laid back, hey-ho way. "I'm just a junkie. I wasn't hurting anyone. Only myself. I just . . . I'd go into rehab, but." They've got him for six years. Six years in prison, he can't see any way out of it. Well, there is a way. "I'll be dead in another town turning somebody in, or I'll be dead in jail." He says this without regret. Mostly, he seems tired. I wonder if he went through withdrawal in jail. Did he stop? The question circles like bees when I look at him. How are you walking around like this? But I don't bring it up. It seems too personal, like asking after an illness.

"It was telling my parents that got me, man. I had to look them in the eye and admit I was a junkie. It did something to me." What he says next is probably what he's had to say to everyone. "I know I did it. I know I fucked up. It's my fault." A big African American guy claps him on the shoulder as he walks past; everyone is on their way to class, and they flow around us like bobbers in a river. "I keep thinking, what could I have done differently? I should have locked the door. I should have kept the cops from getting in."

"It would've happened, anyway."

"It's going to kill me. I won't get back out."

What is there to say when someone tells you that their fate is sealed? I'm sorry.

"If you write," I say, "maybe it will bring you through." What else does he have? But I don't know if Marty knows. There's something hopeless in this guy, something even poems couldn't explain. Hopeless enough to stick a needle into a vein.

"Well." We look at each other. He's so damn small, standing there on the sidewalk, and I know I might not ever see him again, or even hear what becomes of him.

"Hey, try to take care of yourself. Call me. Stop by. Send an e-mail," I say, "but I know, you don't do e-mail," and realize it would be a great option in prison, if they gave prisoners such worldly access. But they wouldn't. We look at each other. There's that moment of not being sure. We're not in class anymore; I give him a one-armed hug. I have books in my other arm. "Keep your soul," I say, though I don't know if that's possible.

He knows what I mean. He nods, but is not convinced. I wouldn't be, either. I pat his shoulder and we part ways and as I walk down the sidewalk in the opposite direction, I feel the undercover cop staring at me, like he knows something. It takes me a day or so to remember that he doesn't know me at all.

back to normal

DEFENDING
THE LAND

AROUND MY AUNT AND UNCLE'S KITCHEN table, the usual Christmas-time talk of dead relatives, jokes, and hunting gave way to the biggest event in the county, ever: Roby Ridge, or the two months that Shirley Allen fought off the State Police. Not only did it put their little town on CNN—it turned my aunt from a dutiful mom-type to a darling of the militia.

The story: Two county deputies tried to serve court papers forcing a fifty-year-old widow to take psychiatric tests. Not in the mood to go, she took a shot at them. The longer Shirley Allen held off the police, the more the standoff attracted the media, which attracted the militia, who took it as their duty to protect her, which attracted more media. Neighbors hovered as close to her yard as they could get—women like my Aunt Teresa, trying to be helpful, and, later, the men. It was backwoods honor; the way they saw it, an isolated country woman was being invaded by relatives who were using legal force to steal her land. The mental testing, they believed, was just an excuse to lock her away.

"If the cops are going to take our homes, we have to fight," said my aunt, explaining why she went past police roadblocks day after day and Shirley Allen had been right to take on armed officers.

"Any of them come to my house, I'm getting out my rifle." My uncle squinted at me, expecting a challenge.

"Teresa was in *People*," my mom beamed proudly, lifting her old green coffee cup. "And *Newsweek*. I have the clippings."

"The militia guys call me all the time. I still get letters. Here, I'll show you." My aunt got up from the dining room table and went into the office put together for the construction business they ran for thirty years. It was the same room where my cousins and I played with matchbox cars and armless Barbies through cooped-up winters.

"Those fellas are pretty nice," nodded Uncle Wade. "Regular folks." One of his grandchildren crawled on his lap and reached for my cousin's wife's peanut butter fudge.

"Nice?" I tried not to raise my eyebrows too far. "They blew up the federal building in Oklahoma. They kill people."

"Oh, that wasn't *these* militia." My uncle shifted Calla, hair a mass of long blond curls, onto his other knee. His belly, expanded from years of Budweiser, was the cushion she leaned against.

"Look." Teresa came out waving a letter; her hair was carefully curled, and for Christmas she wore juniper-colored slacks with a maroon blouse. She flourished the paper in front of me.

The letterhead was a computerized drawing of a revolutionary soldier in a tri-cornered hat, holding a rifle, facing the name "Southern Illinois Patriots League." The graphic reminded me of a bumper sticker plastered on my grandpa's car for three decades: *America, put your heart in it or get your ass out of it.* The sticker had a picture of a donkey; it took me years to figure out why you'd need to get your mule out of the country. With the riots and protests and disorders, the vets in my family were certain they were the only ones left who would protect the land.

Growing up in south-central Illinois, time was an expanse broader than the cornfields. Change was always resisted. I never would have predicted my aunt a protester, let alone a militant. She was kind, even-tempered, kid-centered—a good '60s stay-at-home mom. Roby, Illinois, was not a place for rebels; without the support of family, without education and skills, with children to feed, where was the choice? This town of fifty planted among soybeans allowed people who didn't own suits the means to a cheap and comfortable existence. People in Roby minded their own business. Never put on airs. Were deferential to teachers, bankers, police. What terrified them was what lay beyond the crisp yellow horizon. All the problems inside—the drinking, sudden pregnancies, beatings, accidents—were just a part of the way it was, no big deal, could be handled. Family stuck through everything.

So the idea that a family feud could evolve into a police

back to normal

action big enough for CNN was ridiculous, like something in one of those postmodern novels of fragmentation and conspiracies and ironies and political intent. Nothing this absurd, this *contemporary*, could happen in my little town, which had always imploded with the silent pains of individual homes and the toughness of rural coping. We made do. We held together. When we didn't hold, we went on and didn't complain. We gathered tools of survival—hoes, knives, hammers, spoons, guns—and knew how to use them.

Shirley Allen, a former nurse, knew that forced placement on the psychiatric ward meant drugs and imprisonment, so she responded with the strongest resources at her disposal: a shotgun poised out a window, provisions that would last for weeks, and her own skills as a country kid, which allowed her to shoot straight, think connivingly, and maintain.

The locals, like always, had a line of scuttlebutt—the "real scoop," as opposed to what was said in the papers. My relatives claimed the woman was badgered: The police killed her dog. Cut down her trees to get a better view of her house, then taunted her with the reminder that her dead husband had planted those trees. Kept her from sleeping. Planted lies in the press. Planned to burn her out. The reported facts: The police tapped her phone, cut off her power, broke out her windows, clipped the wires to her well (leaving her without water or sewer service), placed microphones and mirrors to her windows to monitor her movements, shot her with rubber bullets, and harangued her over loudspeakers.

Shirley lived in a small ranch home set on forty acres of unfarmable land extending back to the Sangamon River. It was like the house my cousins lived in when they were little, like most of the houses in Roby—inexpensive, generic, with a bay window and a glass door leading to a back deck. Shirley Allen had kept to herself, more or less, since her husband had died of cancer in 1989. She and her husband used to camp, hunt, and ride motorcycles; she was at home in the natural world. Managing her acreage after her husband's death couldn't have been easy, but, according to neighbors, Shirley kept the place nice. Her house was tidy and her yard well-tended, although one justification for the court order was that Shirley had let weeds grow in her flowers. According to her brother, she was paranoid, although this was never borne out by psychiatric tests. She thought some members of her family were out to get her, and so she cut off contact, refusing to visit with them on Labor Day. Her brother and mother said they just wanted to help her. She feared they were after her property, which, like all rural land, had gone up in value.

"What we heard," Teresa told me, "is that for years she supported this brother from Arkansas and then cut him off. He's getting even."

"You can legally steal," my uncle said, with solemn authority. "Just get a judge to do it."

"How do you know that's true, though?" I asked. "Maybe they really are just worried about her."

They all laughed. "Everyone knows it around here."

"But didn't she shoot at the policeman?"

"She didn't shoot *at* him," my aunt grinned. "She shot *past* him! If she'da wanted to kill, she would have! She's been shooting since she was a kid."

"She knew that deputy, the one that served the warrant," Uncle Wade said. "He was my cousin, her neighbor. They lived right down the road. He comes walking up with her brother, who she knows wants to put her away. She closes the door in their face, and what do they do? They lob tear gas through the poor lady's window! Hell, she *had* to take a shot."

"The woman was scared." My aunt's chin had that stubborn, sulking jut, a family trademark: the sign of embattlement that brought on feisty independence that brought on embattlement. Everyone in my family loved a good fight, especially when some black-and-white position was at stake. Though my aunt didn't know Shirley Allen, she believed she was doing the necessary thing in the face of a great wrong. Whether she was defending the principle of freedom, or the rights of this woman, or the last stand against invasion by the city finally didn't matter. She was willing to go to any lengths; like the heroes in my uncle's Zane Grey books, a real American takes a stand for the freedom to own and the freedom to be alone.

The grandchild slid off my uncle's lap. Wade went in to get a beer. My aunt touched my shoulder. "It wasn't right," she said.

Country people fall back on distant neighbors. Not often, because they cherish self-sufficiency; but they know that in a real emergency, someone will help. In a place like Roby, you could have gone to school with the person in the accident, or had the victim's mom as a Sunday School teacher, or been talking to the poor guy at the grocery store just yesterday. Even if they didn't like each other—which was often the case—there was the shared recognition of Being From There, with generations of relatives all around, neighbors who knew everything about you and would imagine what they didn't know. This smothering rope of connection pulled them out in a pinch.

So when Shirley Allen barred the door, the tough, silent, mind-your-own-business former Appalachians stood behind her. When police cut off food, water, gas, electricity, and sewer service, the renegade citizens of the county came to the road-block. When police harangued her from a bullhorn every fifteen minutes, then assaulted her with bad music, neighbors made protest signs. Their privacy, too, had been invaded; the noise from the loudspeaker could be heard a half-mile away. The U-shaped road Shirley lived on was barricaded; neighbors were forced to leave their homes, and only people with houses up the drive and their relatives were allowed through the roadblock. There was no mail, no trash pickup. No one, including the press, was allowed near enough the house to view it; a woman who attempted to run groceries to Shirley's front door was arrested when she "entered the bubble."

People who protested—some every day—stood at what police called the "checkpoint area" across from the roadblock. They stood in the rain, holding silent vigils and prayer meetings. The inevitability disturbed them as they remembered a relative who'd been laid off, gotten sick, lost insurance, couldn't get an ambulance, couldn't get to town to buy food.

Local taverns sold t-shirts to raise money for Allen's potential legal fees: "What would you do if it were you?" the shirts asked. The newspaper quoted locals whose attitudes changed over those two months from caution about Shirley Allen's mental state to radical anger at her persecution. Shellie Jacobs, who ran Del's Popcorn Shop, said, "I feel, totally, one hundred percent helpless. You can envision yourself in the situation so easily. If they did that to me, I might do the same thing." Mamie Stone, whose house was two hundred yards away, said, "If we treated an animal the way they treated her, we would be arrested." And my aunt, the housewife who raised four kids, told a reporter, "I plan to come out here each night. I want something done. This lady needs heat. She's got to be cold. She's not a criminal."

Since Teresa had relatives up the road (as she did up most roads around there), she was one of the few allowed to drive past the roadblock to, as she put it, "keep an eye on things." She told police she had to visit a sick relative who she actually hadn't talked to in years. This white lie for access was the only time my aunt had broken, or even stretched, the law.

I had broken most of the laws of my childhood, doing what country girls were never supposed to do: get an education, live in town, hold a job, get a divorce, raise a child alone. My aunt would never have rejected the family this way. I wasn't around when my relatives fought the law; I heard about it through long-distance conversations and the news. On my nineteen-inch TV I found Roby, the town where my cousins and I grew up bike-riding on

back to normal

back roads and climbing dirt piles and swinging on tires—Roby, not even big enough for a convenience store. Twenty houses and a church. Flat, stark land in all directions and the winding narrow part of the Sangamon River. Railroad tracks, country music, and fishing poles, girls on horses and men who wielded belts when the bad mood took them. My childhood wanderings through the woods were balanced by the strictness of our behavior inside the house. We were supposed to behave, and this meant being good girls and tough boys. I was considered the family troublemaker, a potential corruptor of my younger cousins because I read too much and thought I was smart and didn't act like a girl. My cousin Brenda, after all, had a pink room and had to wear dresses every day. I climbed trees, dug holes, played with trucks along with Barbies, and could have cared less about fashion. This wasn't to say my cousins were always obedient. Like squirrels, we learned to be mischievous and sneaky and to run and hide when necessary.

The rules were there for self-protection. The folks were afraid that it would end: their property, freedom, money, way of life. Even knowing how strongly my relatives felt about land and ownership, it was hard to make the leap from card table conversation about errant presidents to actual shooting at police who invaded private property. The answer had to be in the place. The wooden bridge down the back road, the thatch of woods behind my cousins' house, the gravel pit a mile down, dogs and boys and secrets and rages and *Modern Confessions* and square dances. Sun on sticky tar and crunch of ice beneath sled runners. Riding a bike for an hour and not passing even one car.

Anyone not completely assimilated *country*—line dancing, vegetable raising, horse breaking, beer drinking, joke telling— was, to them, suspicious. They were right to be worried. While a store would never sell a book with an epithet announcing it to be an African American cookbook, and put an Aunt Jemima character on the front, I found a white trash cookbook with a fat white woman on the cover with a flour bag shirt and greasy hair. White trash magnets with plaid tablecloths and jars of Miracle Whip hold lists of daily appointments. *The Beverly Hillbillies,* the story of a rural family that couldn't adapt to city life, amuses us with its very idea: hicks in Los Angeles. (It's hard to imagine Dust Bowl migrant workers seeking the sunny life and getting poverty finding this all that funny.) *Country* means in-bred, uneducated, ignorant, poor, backwards. Their reaction to the outsider's conception of them would be to flash the bird outside the window of a shiny pickup hauling lumber. Unlike the show-off, gas-hog, pointless SUVs of suburbanites, the farmer's truck is a tool. After giving city folks the finger, they'd go home and hide among family. Because they can't fit, country people laugh at the social web beyond their fields and hope their children will reject it, too.

Beyond the truck, rows of corn, jeans, and dialect was a rural world as complicated as the urban pinball maze. So many natural necessities, like bringing in the crops or constructing a house before the snow. People hid their feelings; joking substituted for handshakes. The manners didn't transfer; our ways were so different from the city's that we couldn't communicate there. We knew the cycles of planting and the labyrinth of gossip at the gas station, but nothing of the proper designer dress to wear to the insurance company picnic. This difference might have been fine except that the structures of power lay in the maneuverings of the city, not in the ability to build a shed, dry herbs, or can beets. All the country person had was the personal plot of land, and as the land was bought up by big companies, as city people moved to the expanding suburbs or saw the profit in the conglomerate farm, even the land seemed impossible to keep.

"That deputy should never have served that warrant to begin with." My uncle smashed a fist on the table. None of us jumped. "Sometimes you don't do your job. There's a line you don't cross."

I stared at Wade. Radical disobedience from Mr. Obey-or-

back to normal

Die? From the man who thought all rebelling college students should be kicked out of school or shot, who thought war resisters should be tossed on the front lines as commie bait? But it was okay if it supported my uncle's version of America. To my uncle, democracy was the freedom to own and to protect what was owned: land, livestock, TVs, children, wives. *Little pink houses for you and me.* Shot burglars and shot adulterers were not uncommon. Why not shot cops?

"They tapped our phone," claimed my uncle.

"You could hear the clicks," added Teresa.

"The militia guys wouldn't even talk on our line. This was right before the rally."

"We kept them up on what was really going on. The police thought we were all big conspirators." My uncle grinned like a hound dog, his Clark Gable face folding into weathered wrinkles.

"We weren't, though," Teresa said, to make sure I understood. "We were just there to help this woman, not to overthrow the government. Although—" She nodded, and my relatives laughed.

"They piped in Barry Manilow music." My uncle gave a shiver. "What did they think she was, an idiot?"

"It wasn't just music, though. It was talking and static and all this loud bass stuff. Said they were trying to calm her down. They were trying to drive her crazy."

I imagined Shirley cringing under her bed, barraged by multiple playings of "I Write the Songs." "That would do it for me," I admitted.

More stories. My aunt, hands in her jacket pockets, trying to persuade the police to let her bring the woman water. My cousin Kirk sneaking his car around the roadblock, then driving to the back of the woman's house to see if there were "booby traps."

"We were afraid they'd bomb her or shoot her through her windows." Teresa poured everyone more weak coffee from the pink-flowered carafe.

DEFENDING THE LAND

"But they didn't."

"No. But that's just because we were there."

I'd been down Shirley's road a few times as a kid, visiting my cousins' cousins' ramshackle house. A family of twins—two sets—with uncontrolled curly hair, and I had a crush on the oldest boy, the only one not twinned, who trained horses. We were both too awkward to do anything about our attraction. He never went to college and I did; he still gets paid to break horses. I'd been amazed by the hickness of their place, even compared to my own; their cabin had a broken-slatted wooden porch and was full of old banjos and guitars and a scarred upright piano. The couches and chairs had hand-crocheted throws to hide the holes. Dogs and cats and kids ran everywhere. Up a hill, down a dirt road, a tire swing in a tree, rusted toys scattered across the dirt, and I loved it: the mess, the tough twin girls, the games played in the dusty yard. My mom grew up just this way, with only one doll in her life until her cousin bashed it on the ground and it shattered, being china. My mom bought my daughter porcelain doll after doll until Paige didn't even bother to name them.

Down that same winding back road lived Shirley Allen. Roby was for people who needed privacy, who wanted to accumulate junk and thoughts. It was nothing like the orderly subdivisions on the outskirts of cities: no white picket fences, two-car garages, or architecturally designed A-frames. These were cabins, trailers, and one-story houses that popped up cheaply and were kept within the family. Shirley Allen stayed down that back road because she wanted to hide. It was the one thing she was not allowed to do. It was, in fact, why the police came to her door.

"So why didn't she just come out and take the tests?" This, to me, was the obvious question, but my relatives seemed surprised to hear it.

"She was afraid they'd shoot her, what with all those guns leveled at her house."

"Maybe she just didn't want to," said my aunt. "Maybe she

back to normal

decided to hell with it. That's what I would've done. Somebody come to my house like that, without a warrant, looking for me or one of my kids, I would've blown them away."

What could I say to that vision of Aunt Teresa standing on the front stoop with a rifle in her hands, except that I believed it? There were plenty of guns around. I'd watched the women skin animals after hunting, handling the pink flesh of cute bunnies—headless, skinless bunnies—with bellies and strong splayed legs.

She'd do it, all right.

"Now listen up about the rally." Everyone sat straighter. This was the most exciting thing that ever happened in Roby. There were two militia protests: one in Taylorville, a factory town of twenty thousand, and another in Mt. Auburn, a dying burg not much bigger than Roby. Members of the major U.S. militia groups made guest appearances: the Militia of Montana, the Southern Illinois Patriots League, the Michigan Militia. One camper flew the American flag upside down; "the international sign," my uncle said, "of distress." Buses and vans carried warriors from as far away as California; the visitors represented, according to the license plates, most of the western states, along with the Ozark territories. Roby became their post-Waco, post–Ruby Ridge cause.

October. Everyone was worried, edgy. Shirley, heat shut off, might freeze. Nearly two months, and she still wouldn't come out, though she was spotted moving past her windows. The newspaper reported when she was "agitated"; it reported when she slept. Psychologists conjectured about her mental illness. The public debated paranoia, patients' rights, community protection, the militia, and the State Police. As time went on, sympathy shifted to Shirley.

She survived off the provisions all rural people kept in their basements: pickles and preserves, bulk grains, bottled water. The question became how much she had. In the country, some people stock up, since in a disaster power may be out, wells may be dry, roads blocked. A woman alone, she was prepared. People in isolation get robbed or worse, so she had weapons: a shotgun, an antique pistol, and a handgun.

But she couldn't last forever. What would the police do to save face? If they lobbed chemicals through her windows and rubber bullets at her body, would they get tired and burn her out, the way they had with radical groups from Move to the Symbionese Liberation Army? Why had everything gotten so quiet?

Something Was Going to Happen.

The militia claimed they were there to prevent it. Their presence, they said, cautioned police against taking action. Atrocity happened in a vacuum; only a public outcry could stop it. The militia dubbed the situation "Roby Ridge," holding up the image of Ruby Ridge and the FBI shooting of a militia family. This town of struggling, stubborn people became a prime media opportunity.

The rallies were proper, contained. Speakers protested the law itself, which permitted court-ordered commitment for mental instability. The law, claimed its detractors, gave an in for disgruntled or greedy relatives or guardians to have people placed into forced psychiatric care. Two legal guidelines existed for committal: an expectation of bodily harm to oneself or others, or an inability to provide self-care. If the person was committed, she could be treated for up to five months before a second hearing determined competency. Essentially, it was the period in prison before trial. What angered the militia were the loss of individual rights and the possibility for abuse or outright theft. Eccentrics or mavericks or the unacceptable, like the secluded, the sick, or the old, could be held against their will.

The rallies were white; the enemy wasn't black (this time), but a government that could take land, money, or guns, could recognize difference and threat and lock them away. Their fear was rational, because they were different and dangerous and knew it. (Shirley was not afraid to fire her gun.) What happened to Shirley Allen could have happened to them or their children—and would in time. They'd be subsumed. Their kids would get ideas and move away to become college professors and writers and architects and bankers. They had already been invaded by people seeking a quiet, suburban life. Now came outrage of the defeated, flying the international flag of crisis. Frontier-minded, they'd go out shooting.

In Mt. Auburn, John Trochmann, founder of the Militia of Montana (one of the largest), defended the right to due process. He said, "Your neighbor's life is at stake. If not hers, yours—sooner or later." A sign from God in the form of a stalled van kept him in Illinois, he said, long enough to speak to the people gathered in Shirley's defense. After the rally, people gave him money, and the previously unconverted found an organization, a mission, that made physical and controlled all the defensiveness that never had so clear a cause.

"Very polite men," said my aunt. As they could see my skepticism, they worked to convince me. The dining room, with its grandfather clock and handmade table, looked very small. Outside the sliding glass doors were the yard and the field beyond. I wanted to be out there. In the swirl of the cigarette smoke, I heard all the angry arguments of my childhood. Some had been directed at me, but most hadn't; the men fought the men, the men fought the women, and the women and men fought us kids in an effort to keep us in line. Always a battle because they were on the losing end. Life never stacked up, yet their biggest fear was that what little they had would be taken away. My life was so different from that of my citified school friends, whose world was linked in a brocade of clubs, stores, restaurants, gyms, yards. I never felt as trapped in their houses as I did in my own. Their neighbors were only a few feet away. The world went beyond their doors and didn't stop at the edge of the field.

Shirley, trapped into hiding behind her bathroom door,

avoided being overcome by the pepper spray lobbed through the windows. Police broke out her sliding glass back door and sent in J.D. She shot J.D., a police dog, in the muzzle. (The dog whimpered, only slightly hurt, though his term as an officer was over.) A few days later, cops pushed food through the door. They reconnected Shirley's power. A fire engine, an ambulance, and the rescue squad were brought in, a move locals feared would predicate a Waco-style burnout. Officers said they were there to protect Shirley in case the restored power ignited something on her stove.

But she never turned on the gas or ate the food. Assuming poisons and drugs, she left the sack on the back porch. She carried out another sack. That was when she fell in a barrage of rubber bullets.

Her brother and stepdaughter applauded Shirley's safe delivery onto the psychiatric floor of St. John's Hospital.

On the TV news, Shirley, declared sane, talked. Lining the shelves of her small house were books: literature, psychology, history. This studiousness was a surprising, very un-Roby-like thing about Shirley Allen, who looked like a nice, thoughtful, aunt-ish sort of person. Fifty-something, brown hair, glasses, and a wry sense of humor. With those books, no wonder her relatives thought she was crazy, I told my fiancé. He laughed, but I meant it.

No one needed schooling because it had no purpose. One exception was Shirley Allen, with her nursing degree and her hardback books and her dial tuned to the public radio station (the police reported everything after they'd searched the house, from its physical condition—tidy—to the radio dial). It was only after she'd been besieged for weeks that the locals came to see Shirley as just like them, your average country girl.

Like my cousin who swore his daughters would never visit Chicago ("only if you carry a gun!"), the farm folks' deepest fear was that Chicago would visit them. It used to be in the form of intruders with darker skin colors, with tie-dye and advanced degrees. Now their phantoms were uniformed men. Shirley, claimed by her country cousins and patriot mentors, became a heroine who defied intrusion. She kept her property, and replaced her windows. According to the local gossip, she returned to her hermetic ways, and she always trims her rose bushes.

growing up with
with
rednecks and
punks

PAINTED BIRD, SANGAMON COYOTE

A PONY WAS LED IN A CIRCLE on the patch of land that would later become our backyard. When I was that young, I looked beyond the pony's mane and saw how the land sloped unobstructed in all directions. I, a Phoenix child, felt dropped into desolation very different from cactus and sand. It was me, the horse, and Grandpa, who led us on a rope, barking directions that the Shetland never hesitated to obey. I held onto both rein and white straw mane, my rear end sliding on the animal's bare back. "What, think you're gonna fall?" Grandpa taunted. "No kid related to me would fall off a puny little *pony*." Over time, the land around our country property became constricted by so many subdivisions that our rural route became a street. And I did fall off and get kicked in the head. Losing interest, Grandpa sold the pony, which he had taught to kneel.

My family moved to my grandparents' land when I was nine; Grandma and Grandpa lived in a black A-frame behind us. Their acre extended to the Sangamon River, home of summer catfish. Behind my grandparents' house was the timber and river-bottom soil that began on the top of a hill and then sloped to the water. Beneath the sassafras trees was a fertile sandpile where we kids dug as we chose, driving our small metal shovels around roots. This circle of dirt became the Sahara, gravesites, the Indianapolis 500, and a potential route to freedom, which was on the opposite end of the earth.

When I was very young, Grandma and Grandpa's water was drawn from a hand pump and they had a rusty ineffective toilet in an unfinished room little bigger than a closet. My brother and I took baths together in a shiny metal tub into which Mom poured boiling water mixed with cold. Grandpa kept the newsprint magazine *Grit* on the toilet; Grandma's doorless bathroom shelves were lined with foot creams and Tucks and a powder puff, but no perfume. Not even Avon.

My childhood was put together in bits and pieces. Much of what we needed we made by hand. Grandpa was a builder who controlled design and execution. He constructed the form of our family. He'd sit at our kitchen table, smoking George Burns cigars, which he'd tap on the glass ashtray while bragging, ranting, gossiping. The carpenter, the poker player, the guy who could keep his car running for twenty years, was pals with half the county. His mind was quick and he let you know it; to hear him tell it, he was the smartest guy around, and would've been the most successful, too, if life hadn't gotten in the way. "I met Bette Davis when I was in the service. Had a drink together in this bar in California. A dress slit up to her thigh and could she tell a joke!" (He told this tale so many times I think it may be true.) Or "I knew so much about math in high school I had to help out the teacher. He finally set me up to teach the class myself." (Grandpa figured the angles for houses, furniture, and the bridge that spanned the ravine.) Or "I was telling Jim down at the tavern about them goddamned Republicans and how I kicked that bastard out of office." Mom, Grandma, and my aunt and uncle nodded, pretending interest because no one wanted to insult him and send him into a tirade that would end in weeks of cold silence. "That's just the way he is," they sighed in the kitchen or on the porch. I never knew what they meant. I envied his life outside our country houses; that he could know so much, so many people.

Sometimes he'd take us into Springfield. Always to Kmart on Clear Lake, and Bud's Red Fox Grocery across from the trailer park where Aunt Billie lived. Grandpa's reception in these places was proof to me that he really was a man about town—I didn't know at the time that it was the wrong side of town.

At Kmart, he knew Jenny, the fat woman behind the returns counter, and Julie, a mousy girl, maybe a little slow, who wore metal clips in her scraggly hair. There was Randy who worked in Shoes, and Craig, manager of Housewares. Grandpa would call out to them so that everyone would turn, and the clerks in their blue smocks would come and talk, glad to get a chance to goof off. I'd take that opportunity to escape to the book section, where I'd flip through the kid novels with cardboard covers, *The Partridge Family Goes to Rome,* or *Tracy Belden, Girl Detective.* If I had a few bucks, I'd pick up a *Tiger Beat* and then slide over to the record section and pick out a ninety-nine-cent single. Grandpa thought this was a waste of good money that ought to be kept in a bank and saved for something useful like a decent second-hand car. "Entertainment, that's all you kids want," he'd complain, while going over to the cigar section to pick out his Tiparillos. The tobacco aisle, which was sectioned by the Icee machine, smelled like cherries, men and cherries. I'd pick up the pouches of pipe tobacco and sniff, wishing I had the kind of dad who wore tweed.

At Bud's Clear Lake Food Mart, Grandpa's reputation was even more secure. My cousins and I loved these trips, because we were allowed to raid the shelves for SweeTarts and candy lips. He'd wave his wallet and introduce the five of us and tell Maggie, Bud's wife, about all the stuff he bought us that he never did, and we'd stand among the candy with the black city kids, who we would eye with curiosity but never speak to, for we'd been raised to be afraid of them. They always seemed okay to me—shy, in fact, like they weren't so sure what we'd do to them, and they'd defer sometimes, moving on down the aisle in a way that made me want to apologize. The girls often had on lightweight frocks and black shiny shoes, and I wondered why they needed to dress up like that and show off their money.

As we went through the line to pay, Grandpa told the cashier each of our names and our separate achievements. I was the smart one; Mike the practical one; Sissy was pretty; Joey, an imp; and he tended to skip my poor brother, who was overweight and, to the family, as dreamy and useless as my dad.

While Grandpa built himself and us up, he needled us kids the way many men like to tease children. A pimple, a lost tooth, a stutter, a bad haircut were all grist for one-liners. I grew up sure he knew social secrets I'd never be able to pull off—secrets that I, morbidly shy, found as mysterious as a tomb. There seemed something dark in it, as if being the jokester and the popular one must involve some deep lie, a selling of the soul. The more I wanted to know how to talk to everyone in non-stop bluster the way Grandpa did, the less I was able to do it. "You just got to open your mouth," he'd say, pointing with that cigar. "Open that trap and put your foot down. No need to spend life being a shrinking violet. Somebody's going to step on you, kid." Didn't I know it. But all I could do was smile and shrug, wishing I could just not care what people thought, the way Grandpa did. It took me forever to see that it was all he lived for.

Our Phoenix desert days had ended when my uncle, who lived with us back then, died of a brain tumor and my dad had a nervous breakdown and was going to lose his job at the Salt River Project. So we traveled back to Illinois and spent two years in the town of Buffalo down the road from my grandparents. Finally, Mom cut a deal with Grandpa to live in and slowly pay for his old house. (They had built the new A-frame for them-selves in the backyard so that we could move onto this property.) This made my mother happy—she liked being secluded. I saw it as being permanently grounded. I went from being a city child in a multi-colored neighborhood, to an outsider in an all-white pin-spot town, a lone hick in the vast country of nowhere. No neighbors, no friends to hang out with, no freedom. Since they lived so close, my grandparents watched my every kid move, making it difficult to get into the standard trouble. Nature looked to me like a lot of boring trees. I saw nothing to do, no one to talk to, no purpose—always under the big family thumb.

Our new house was full of Grandpa's idiosyncrasies: there was one long half-basement room with a cement floor that served as living room and kitchen. The windows were level with the ground, so that, watching TV, we would look up at flowers through one pane and the dog's nose pressed against another.

growing up with rednecks **and** punks

The kitchen window showed the breezeway; the glass kitchen door, a flight of steps. Natural light was hard to come by. But I liked the coziness of my mom working in the kitchen while my brother and I, stretched out on the living room rug, watched *Bonanza* or *I Dream of Jeannie*—all of us in the same unseparated space. That wasn't the only quirky feature. The kitchen had an ancient black cookstove that was used sometimes in the winter for heat, and a round legless table permanently attached to the wall. Above the table was a roll-up door behind which we kept notepads for card scores, and pens and pencils and rubber bands and hair ties. Whatever my father would break or put in backwards, Grandpa would fix in minutes. He loved showing all of us how to do things right. The hell of it was, when it came to getting things to work, he *was* always right.

Up a few steps from the kitchen was the breezeway. This room connected house to garage, where we kept the freezer, and my brother and I set up our race-car track on its cement floor and played village. Only one artistic note marred the utilitarian scheme: on the wall was a delicate pink and black painting my grandparents had done of a cockatoo-like bird in a gilded cage. It strikes me as odd now that this should be there, since they had done no other painting, ever. But I loved that bird, often catching its eye on the way in from outside. It reminded me of my grandparents, who I had always felt more comfortable around than my own parents, though Grandpa had a nasty temper. As a kid, I felt reassured by his wheezing emphysemic cough: he was around, on the move, getting things done.

Grandpa had other hobbies. He made miniature wooden carts and buggies attached to carved horses. He cooked chili and, on holidays, oysters. He fished and taught me to fish. "Teed," his nickname was, because he was always teed off; his real name was Leo, the lion. Hawk-nosed, he was as precise as the angles of his thin, olive-skinned body. "One hand there," he said, demonstrating with his fishing rod. "Hold it down. Swing back, over the shoulder, but only this far. This far, not that far, damn it. Right, that's right, right there; and then you arc it, you see, so that it floats over there. There, you understand that," and his line would sail far over bank and stumps and out into the center of our river, catching in the current. "Then you turn, here, and pull in your line, so it's taut. And keep that eye on the end of that pole." But I already knew that. I'd watched lines my whole childhood. I had a cane pole when I was eight, moved to a rod and reel before I was twelve, had no fear of plunging the hook through the body of an earthworm. Wasn't much bothered by the worm goo which I'd wipe off from my fingers onto the grass. I was fascinated by the way the worm kept wriggling, even after it should have been mortally stabbed; I wondered if it was that they never died. They seemed such a different eyeless species that I figured maybe they didn't play by our rules.

Once I learned to cast, I fished from the upper bank like the grown-ups, instead of the lower where the short line on my cane pole reached the water. This was a passage to responsibility, since rods and reels were expensive and complex, and the chances of snagging greater given all the space the line had to travel. For the line sailed instead of plunked, demonstrating the distance between grown-up possibilities and the limits set upon us kids. With casting came the whirr of the reel, the definitive click when setting it. And I got to have my own red-metal rod holder instead of the forked stick we used on the lower bank.

Through fishing I was not only allowed to enter the realm of the adult, I got to be like a boy. My mom had her own rod, but didn't fish much; Aunt Teresa and Grandma didn't at all. Instead, they made coffee and Kool-Aid and brought it out on trays, then sat in the shade to chat and watch. I don't know why Grandpa chose to teach me rather than my cousin Mike or my brother Tony. I like to think that he saw potential, that he knew I could fish in a way that the boys couldn't.

No one spent more time at the river than I. Mostly, I used the

growing up with rednecks and punks

pole as an excuse to laze away the day reading in the sun. I became acquainted with Dostoyevski, Mario Puzo, Anne Tyler, the Brontës—absorb awhile and daydream it over. How Grandpa could figure this as being anything like his way of country is surprising, given the needling I got about always having my nose in a book. Yet it took me only two tries before my line arced into the current, and I pulled it taut and set the rod in the holder like some grizzled pro. Grandpa didn't give me a bit of encouragement. "Loosen up your arm," he said. "But not so low there behind you. Watch me." And he reeled in his line and cast again, just to make his point, lest I for a moment thought I might have something on him. And, of course, his went farther and didn't drift like mine toward the tree roots knotted around the bank like arthritic nature hands.

Like everyone in my family, Grandpa worked nearly all the time, painting the house, fixing the car, building an addition, making furniture, pruning trees. His only relaxation came from listening to Cardinals games on the transistor radio and playing poker and going down to the tavern late in the evening.

We were rarely shown the drinking side of his life, though sometimes for an afternoon he'd take us grandkids to the Sandbar for a lunch of burgers, American fries, and jukebox music. The tavern housed Grandpa's second existence, one in which Grandma never took part.

It's easy to miss the obvious when love is involved. It isn't our affection or its object we're protecting, but our sense of self. If we admit that the cared-for one isn't all we believed him to be, then we must face our own blindness. If that person is a patriarch, a matriarch, a betrayer, a bully, then we become implicated. With the desperate need to get along, it's hard to accept truths. Everything from annoying quirks to crazy derangements are as taken-for-granted as the brand of peas served with the Sunday pot roast. For a child, it's all just lowered-bar normal. There must be an intrusion before we can see—a friendly visitor, a natural storm, a new place, a stranger. My family avoided these.

College was a new universe: I got out of the house and the town and into the city. I had city friends, went to city bars, and listened to unusual music. I became daring. I had questions and asked them. I thrived on walking alone into forbidden places, and if people didn't like it, to hell with them. I got a little wild.

But I wasn't tough. Not as tough as my family thought I was. I saw myself as an explorer. They saw me as a rules-breaking whore who should be married and spitting out kids. I didn't know how to take this. Was my family over-protective, loving, and concerned, misunderstanding because I was the first to go to college? Or were they mean, violent, looney, semi-literate assholes? And was there an in-between? Fury, which had always sparked under my skin, hadn't erupted yet into full-blown prairie fire. I was still feeling generous. I was having too much fun.

I tried to leave my family behind, like closing a book after creasing the page. You can always go back. But it's hard to live in two worlds. I kept losing my place.

I had wanted to go away to school, but Mom needed me to stay. She wasn't ready to be alone with my dad and brother and had no good job yet to draw her attention. She tried to persuade me to take a full-time job, but I fought this, knowing if I did I'd probably *never* go to college. Since there was no money, I worked side jobs to pay for tuition and gas. I didn't know how to make the break.

So I kept walking into reality. Driving home one evening, I was hit by a whim. Every day I drove past the Sandbar Tavern, a pleasant watering hole on the blacktop between our house and Springfield, and more often than not Grandpa's car was there. I did something I'd never done before.

I pulled into the gravel parking lot among the rusted pickup trucks and dull Chevies. When I opened the tavern's creaking screen door, I found a lineup of men hunched at barstools. It took me awhile to pick out my grandfather's narrow back, his blue Arrow shirt. I avoided looking anyone in the eye. I wasn't sure why I'd come; some moment of nostalgia, wanting to be accepted as a friend, an equal. Except in a tavern women are pick-ups until proven otherwise. But I was dumb; I was thinking back to when I was a kid and Grandpa would take us to the Sandbar for Sunday catfish and waffled fries. Red checkered tablecloths and a jukebox stocked with Elvis and Buck Owens and Patsy Cline.

Above our heads, a team of Budweiser horses circled in a white globe lamp. Behind the bar the usual mirror showed tired faces, and in front of the faces rows of spigoted bottles, Jim Beam, peppermint schnapps, Southern Comfort, Gilbey's gin. Sweetness glinted in their shine, their offer of denied candies, adult adventures. I loved bars and still do, right down to a squirmy anticipatory nervousness in my stomach. But I didn't like seeing my grandpa frail and bent, surrounded by a burly tattooed young guy on one side and a harried waitress with cotton-white-bleached hair retrieving a tray of drinks on the other.

"Hey, it's my granddaughter," he said. "Here, pull over that stool." He pointed to the other side of the big guy. I looked at Mr. Tattoo to see if he had dibs. He stared into his shot glass, refusing congeniality. I moved the seat around, creeped out by tavern seediness, that sense of things ripening in dark corners. But I had a macho streak, determined to ignore hesitation to take things through to an end.

"Let me order you a beer," Grandpa said, too loudly. He waved his arm at the bartender, a woman with ratted red hair and drawn-on eyebrows the shape of wood staples.

I didn't really want a beer. Maybe it was Tammy Wynette wailing on the jukebox; I felt like one of those women who listened to sad country songs and cheated on their men.

The draft Miller came down in front of me. My grandfather

introduced me to Mr. Tattoo, the son of someone who hauled sand and gravel. The guy, who wasn't much older than me, clapped an arm around Grandpa's shoulder. "Yeah, Leo is quite a fella. He's done a million things in his life, right, Leo? Won World War II on his own, slept with movie stars, built a mansion." He smirked.

Everyone knew my grandfather was a bullshitter. More than that, a liar. In the family we learned not to listen. Or maybe I half believed he really did have friends all over the county, and everyone depended on him and he was the smartest in his class.

But in the bar, none of these many friends came up to talk to my grandpa.

"What else you do, huh, Leo? Build the White House or something?"

"That's right." Maybe he believed, by this time, that he had done these things. He'd begun wandering off over the past year; his hand trembled so much that he couldn't sign his name. "That's it, goddamn it. I designed Wayne Park's house. That mansion, out on 36. Didn't get credit for it. Everyone was jealous."

The guy, whose name was Mark, kept it up, trying to impress me. I'd never seen my grandfather, a man of pride and incredible temper, treated this way. Everyone in the family did what he wanted. But now I saw an old man who didn't fight, who maybe didn't even know he was being made a fool.

I should've felt a twinge of winning. He'd pushed us around with his impatient rages, his imperious know-it-all attitude. But I felt robbed; I'd lost the man who built the house. If Grandpa was only a small man, a dispatcher for Nabisco, a tavern drunk, then what was I?

My life was boundaried by river and fields. Still, I thought I was better than all that, or that all of it was better than I knew it to be in terms of status. I wanted to like it for what it was. Closing my eyes to ambition, I was going to a community college.

growing up with rednecks **and** punks

Grandpa had never become a math teacher, which was what he wanted to be; instead, he raised three kids and snuck us home free boxes of Nabisco Oreos and Lorna Doones.

I wanted Grandpa to show this redneck that he was better than a joke. Instead, he turned to me. His words slurred. Many nights he must've come home smashed and never shown it. Maybe he went off to bed on those nights or fell asleep in front of the TV. Or maybe he had gotten old.

I drifted to the juke box music, the Oak Ridge Boys singing "Elvira," a song I hated because it ripped off an old Leiber/Stoller tune. The TV flipping the news, Dan Rather on bad reception. Jimmy Carter smiling his peanut smile, everything silly and hopeful.

"Your grandma snared me, you know. If it hadn't been for her I would've done something. But she tricked me. How women do. Got herself knocked up. Made me get her a ring. I had to do the honorable thing, but if I hadn't it would've been something else. Now I bought her that new ring, it put me back a few hundred, with all the stones in it and she ought to be glad for it. I stayed all along but there she trapped me. . . ."

I guess he thought since we were in a bar, and that made me an adult, I could hear all this. Or more than likely he didn't think. Like I cared about his life, his failure.

It was what men want and what they can't have. All that was never said in my family. A family of hypocrites I wanted to see through, feel righteous about; yet here was just this old skinny mean-hearted man not worth bothering with.

"She tricked me," he kept saying. "I come around now, I'm there, but let's face it."

I wish I could say I talked back, defended Grandma. But I just thanked him for buying me the beer. I had that dizzy claustrophobic feeling and knew I'd made a hideous mistake. I couldn't go back to seeing the little bar as a place with fried Saturday catfish and cokes with crushed ice. It was sour beer and a frazzled waitress and people with no place to go, or no place they wanted to go.

So what happens when you get to the end? I went from loving him as a child to assessing betrayals and deceptions just as we might some abandoned lover or life. The need to swing a wide arc to deny his power made it easy to label him. Especially before he died, as his hold dissipated and we kids grew older and stronger and the women got jobs.

After his stroke, the relief in my family was so palpable that none of us cried when we looked in on his casket; we told jokes. This might be seen as my family's usual way of stepping around a crisis, a version of an Irish wake, except we weren't really sad. A little regretful, maybe, nostalgic; but not sad. Sad, tragic, was the day when my cousin Mike's baby daughter was buried—that was a funeral of grief and regret. At Grandpa's ceremony the littlest kids, my cousins' children and my own daughter, peeked into the open casket, touching his bloated hands and jumping back with squeals, running in circles and giggling. Nobody stopped them. Grandma cried, but I couldn't help but wonder whether she'd be rejoicing at her freedom to come and go as she pleased for the first time in her life. I cried, but not for what I'd miss. I didn't cry out of joy for finally being past his sexual gibes at what he saw as my promiscuity. (Sex with a boyfriend outside of marriage was too independent for a man whose daughters all married by the age of seventeen.) I didn't dance for being free of his casual right to humiliate me for being a tough-minded girl. I laughed at the kids, whose lives might be different from mine; I looked with some regret at his two daughters, my mother and aunt, who had given up their possibilities so that they could raise children and be nice. Nope, I cried for losses entirely foolish: moss identification and mushroom hunting.

Grandpa and I and my mom used to drive around the back roads until we got to a timberland. Some old acquaintance of

Grandpa's owned this depth of trees with dark trunks planted closely together so that in the summer only a dappling of sunlight came through the leaves. The smell was rich and musty, damp on the skin and peculiarly mysterious in its dusky silence. We parked his old beige Buick at the side of the road and traversed these woods, carrying sacks, our shoes sinking into the soft dirt and moss. We hunted mushrooms. Not the white kind like hats, because those would kill you. No, these were brown-speckled, cone-shaped mushrooms. Climbing over the barbed-wire fence that snagged our pant legs, walking through the cool woods, looking at the pattern of the scrap of tree bark retrieved from the mud, the bluebells wilting into purple, the white curved petals of miscellaneous no-name flowers so frail that if picked they would not last more than a minute on their thread-thin stalks, the vines that wrapped around a trunk trying to squeeze the life out of something far too old and stubborn to die.

Finding the mushrooms was a game of hide-and-seek in the browns of the woods: distinguishing patterns in the greens and grays—the discovery of what had learned to disguise itself. Nature is bound by its protective markings. Nothing is obvious until the deer is shot, the plant picked. Resistance comes with the ability to blend, to be completely still; listening and seeing are all-important. Instinct, too—a sense of where and when a thing might reveal itself. It might jump out at you, but it might burrow deeper. The forest has pockets of life in every shadow, behind the brambles and the fallen logs. It takes a certain adventurous curiosity, an ability to risk, to find the quiet special things.

If Grandpa had constructed our lives, and we fled and scattered only after he was dead, then maybe we should see what it was that he built. The frame was sturdy but eccentric. Inventive but flawed. It didn't allow for any view but its own, making it functional only for those of like mind. The cool basement living room preceded the earth houses constructed by yuppies; but who but a few would choose to live in the dark? Knowing the right points in the river to run the line would mean nothing to most; but Grandpa's world was very small and as protected as the rabbit's. We were attuned to survival: we could pick berries, can our vegetables, kill squirrels—the old hill ways. We relied on nobody but family and the family had to be kept together by any means. Lies, cajolery, humiliations, paddlings composed the order that kept us within a fifty-mile radius of home. Scattering to the cities was the last resort of only those who couldn't get by. If Grandpa gave up freedom for responsibility, then the rest of us damn well would too. Like the woods plants, we would blend in our silence; we would adapt and behave because it was necessary.

Beneath the trees was moss, green and softer than cloth, cool on the hottest day. Clear of thorns or bees, it was a place to rest. I would sit and watch while the others collected the mushrooms, daydreaming in a way that made me not a very successful survivor in the wild. If Grandpa knew there was no hope for me, he never gave up trying.

He had taught me the country ways; and if these ways meant getting the back of a hand, or being taunted for my stubbornness, or being labeled spoiled for insisting upon college, then I tell you it was worth it for the winter bonfire, the fresh frying catfish, the musty sack of thick-fisted mushrooms, the hard, smooth seed corn scraped off the stalk, lying back into the welcoming leaves or onto a sandy bank or against a rough tree. I learned what Grandma, the orphan, learned: embracing the arrogant untamed gave back the sweet silent breath of the spring day after a rain. The payoff is in the recognition, the ability to cast wider than I ever could have otherwise, and to appreciate the smallest beauties. After blaming, burying the dead, we can only accept that person, that time, for what it was, identify it, praise and damn it, and walk on knowing the difference between the kind of mushroom that'll kill you and the kind that cooks up nice in a stew.

growing up with rednecks and punks

LOST CAUSE
AND SIN

IN CENTRAL ILLINOIS there's always a radio going. Mine stayed defiantly tuned to rock and roll, but the family's stuck to country. Their '60s music had no psychedelic swirls, rebellious rage, or screaming guitars. It was twang with residue lonesome, made for drunken angry workers and rejected, dejected wives. People who didn't have shit.

In the morning, Mom turned on Swap Shop hoping for bargains. I, hanging out in an Illinois sticky summer, watched TV game shows and imagined myself the center star on *Hollywood Squares*. From the kitchen came the dulcet tones of DJ Bruce Bagg, who might trade a broken-down fridge to an eighty-year-old widow who would in turn give up a handmade baby blanket. We kept cool by stretching in front of fans with exposed metal blades.

In the afternoon came a stampede of country hits. Songs between the banging of screen doors, the grabbing of sweet tea, the spatting between my brother and me. Wistful yearning and fierce reactions: Loretta Lynn, George Jones, Patsy Cline, Dolly Parton. I didn't think much of that melancholy melody of entrapment. I figured it had to be better in San Francisco, where hippies wore flowers in their hair, or on Broadway where there were big buildings even if you were down to your very last dime. The honky-tonk songs were just poor people down on their luck with no one to talk to but the stranger listening to their stories of guilt, rejection, and penitence. I'd had enough of this in real life.

Then, about the time I got a serious hankering for boys, country started singing to me. Maybe this had to do with moving from a city, then to a small town, and finally to a river. Loneliness, I found, could be distracted by nature. The singers seemed, like me, entranced by the whispers and moans of treetop breezes. Vulnerable honesty ached in young Dolly Parton's voice as she sang about her coat of many colors and her Tennessee mountain home. To someone with everything, these seem like hard-luck clichés. But they made up Dolly Parton's life and

I recognized it as mine. Mom sewed our clothes because we couldn't afford others; while I couldn't gain Dolly's sense of appreciation for what I had, I found hope in the way Dolly saw it. What's sentimentality but trying to find value in the worst? Loretta Lynn shared Dolly's rough times, but she met hers with anger. Her voice, straightforward and gutsy, dared you not to let her tell it like it is. Where we came from, women and girls weren't supposed to talk back. Yet Loretta advised women to mouth off to men and take the Pill. In a time when even rock-and-roll women were victims, Loretta wasn't. Rock hadn't yet taken on the struggles of home. Rock was the abstract, edgy urban dream; country has always been a place-bound, home-loving skirmish.

Country reflected what I lived with, not what I wanted to be, which was as rowdy as rock and as sensuous as rhythm and blues. Those emotional pining songs were for tired, beaten-down workers. Responsibilities were weights, and there was never enough. Not being middle class meant being a loser. Your kids didn't dress right, you didn't dress right, and you said you didn't care whether you dressed right, but you did. Time in country was endless and futility constant. We carried bulging bags of pride, inflated egos, and enhanced seductions, a noisy cover for futility: He'd leave at the end of the night. The car might get repossessed. Without insurance, the doctor was out. Stand by your man even if he shoves you out the window. Take me back so I can cheat again. Remember Mama and Papa because they sacrificed everything for nothing. Hope someone will remember.

The first country singer I heard was Johnny Cash. Dad played him every Sunday when he loaded the record player with a stack of nostalgia: the Sons of the Pioneers, Phil Harris, Glenn Miller, *Fifty Guitars Go Country*, Roger Miller, and, of course, The Man in Black. That indigo voice spooked my childhood with stories of doomed but honorable losers, like drunken Ira Hayes the Indian Marine, and a hundred trapped cons who

growing up with rednecks **and** punks

erred out of passion. The Johnny Cash album I played most as a kid was the live show at San Quentin, where he did a chilling performance of "Folsom Prison Blues." *When I hear that lonesome whistle, I hang my head and cry. . . .* Rich bankers in the dining car, self doing penance. Surrounded by soybeans, I identified. Drivers went by, accomplishing things, moving on, while I, watched by relatives and small-town busybodies, stayed stuck: awkward, restless, bored, and guilty of being different. Johnny Cash is all about being beset with passions that have to be pulled in. "I Walk the Line." Everybody walks a line.

Cash grew up in Arkansas, where he filled bag after bag with field cotton. I picked corn and beans so we could eat through the summer and freeze food for the winter. Cornstalks were an itchy, grabbing fence, dry and riddled with bugs. The ears weren't always easy to break off, especially if the weather was wet. Husks sliced your hands like paper. Smooth beans, pretty and elegant in their arcing green and zippered seam, grew close to the ground. Picking required bending or stooping, which got your back. Inclined toward books and paintbrushes, heat made me dizzy and the aches increased with the intensity of sun and light. Time crawled through silence, repetition, and the fear that I was doing it wrong and someone would catch me at it. The moment stretched into white glare and painful rhythm, rough dirt against knees and scrapes against hand, snap of stalk, weight of bag. . . . There was no way out. So I engrossed my way into the lash of a spider's leg, the pattern on its plain brown back. Or I lobbed a dirt clod at the back of my brother's head. When Johnny Cash sings about how as an adult he built a life where he "never picked cotton," I remember the heat and I laugh. Given a relative line between fieldwork and luxury, I'm free. Johnny Cash spent a lifetime becoming Johnny Cash so he wouldn't be trapped. I still drift when talking to students, stunned that I'm up there, that I have the right to be heard. In this is the itch of guilt, like the man who cries for what he's done and what he's lost; if I don't finish my job in the field, who will? Do words really count?

LOST CAUSE AND SIN

Guilt drips through country music like beer from a leaking tap. Jilting someone or being jilted because you messed up; drinking too much and screwing up; rejecting someone, meaning you have to pay homage; not dying in the war (any war current or past); being a bad parent and/or prodigal child; taking a crappy job, having a dead-end life. My dad called it "crying music," and swore away from it, except for Johnny; my uncle played it and cried when he got drunk and lined up every lost cause and sin.

An academic once catalogued the themes from Hank Williams's songs: complaint comes up 57% of the time; loneliness, 19%; defiance, 15%; and family, 5%. And the topics?—broken hearts, gospel salvation, hard times, trains, and death. What's funny?—Bad women and hard times. All washed over with remorse and regret. Hank Williams hugged every manifestation of guilt and became the greatest country music artist of all time. And what does guilt come from but failure? Failure to keep commitments, find love, be all you want to be, maintain courage, provide, do or sometimes just know the right thing. It's stricken conscience, the shoring of personal responsibility after collapse. If country music is a long obsession with guilt, what does this say about country people?

No group is a bigger failure. When the American dream was about room to roam and to plant and to harvest, those who lived off the land were the fortunate ones. People referred to the ripening landscapes as "God's country," but as "God's country" turns into industrialists' subdivisions, the phrase has mostly died out. When TV tells us that our ideal American is some nasally upscale *Seinfeld/Frasier/Melrose Place*–like professional, being rural looks awfully anachronistic. No wonder contemporary country music sounds like Celine Dion with a steel guitar or Donny Osmond with a cowboy hat. Nobody's a hillbilly when every hillbilly's got a satellite dish. The encroachment of subdivisions, the loss of the family farm, the growth of cutesy "crafts,"

growing up with rednecks and punks

the suburbanization of small towns, and the derision of anything rural has taken its toll. Country has become mainstream.

Some musicians give in for a buck and fame. Buck Owens held true and then sold his soul, although it's hard to blame him. Owens, from the Okie-transplant city of Bakersfield, sang not about personal losses, but of trying to survive in a redneck haven that squats in paradise. He merged country and rock with the soul of his hillbilly roots; his band, the Buckaroos, built a guitar wall and broke the cliché of the lone and lonely whiskey-drinking singer. For years, Buck told Nashville to go to hell. In songs written thirty years ago, he talks about the town of Bakersfield as if *he* were Bakersfield, and his friends were Bakersfield, and Bakersfield were him. He even spent loads of money on a sign announcing entry into the city. Preservation is what every good Buck Owens song is all about.

But what do I mostly think of when I remember Buck Owens? *Hee Haw*. Buck Sold Out. For The Money. For nineteen years, Owens co-hosted the show that presented country people as the idiots that city people made them out to be. A white trash, whiteface vaudeville riff. Hick humor is all about self-ridicule and neighbor-ridicule, from dirty jokes at the bar to Jeff Foxworthy on TV. The radio used to run long-winded joke records about "catching a bar"—old-fart stories about hunting—and my relatives thought they were funny as hell. These records were top-ten country hits. There were goofy songs, too, like "A Boy Named Sue" and "Running Bear," and everyone went around singing them. Ray Stevens, who started out a pop singer ("Gitarzan" and his jungle band? "Everything Is Beautiful" in its own way? I know all the words to these songs . . . unfortunately), moved his career over to country and just kept cranking them out.

Hee Haw was the tiptop ultra pinnacle of the Yup-Yuck Hillbilly I-Chew-Hay Laugh Riot. *Hee Haw* was the only show my relatives never missed, except for *Bonanza* and the televised

Indy 500. Here's the *Hee Haw* routine: Comics, musicians, and huge-breasted women dressed in overalls and straw hats and ripped shorts would pop up out of a cardboard cornfield and tell asinine jokes. The show's opening credits featured a cartoon jackass. Bad comic skits were broken up by music performed by regulars and "special guests." Nearly every country star did at least one turn in the *Hee Haw* cornfield. In those pre–Nashville Network days, it was one of the few times that country musicians appeared over the airwaves. When people played, the disguises slipped away and their faces got looks of dreamy concentration, as if they were no longer in a studio pretending to be country but out in the hills. Buck Owens shot a year's worth of *Hee Haw* in two weeks and got paid $400,000—not too shabby for a former migrant worker.

Owens didn't act like a hillbilly and was never funny. Fidgety, he seemed out of place among the straw hats and overalls. In his prime, before TV, he and his band wore matching well-pressed suits. The other *Hee Haw* staples—Roy Clark, Minnie Pearl, Grandpa Jones—were Nashville versions of vaudeville entertainers. Nashville's always gone for the cheap, easy, and cornball, and promotes whatever is necessary to Make Money.

Minnie Pearl and Grandpa Jones are just two of the entertainers who changed their names, adopted hokey costumes, and developed a country shtick so that they could become beloved hicks. There's a Minnie Pearl museum in Nashville, full of Minnie's hats with the price tags hanging from them. I went there after viewing Elvis's solid gold Cadillac at the Country Music Hall of Fame. Minnie's museum is weirdly sincere, like visiting an old aunt's attic that is incidentally also offering ten-dollar thermometers. Here's this thin, stately woman with a beautiful face and gentle humor, wearing outrageous sunhats and frilly dresses: the symbol of a hayseed trying so hard to move up that she forgot to remove the tag from her ridiculous hat! Her trademark line was to walk on stage and go "How-DEE!" with this big horsey grin. Yet Minnie has her own museum because, despite looking silly, she had an overriding *dignity*.

After he handed over his musicianship for cash, Buck Owens stopped making good records. The musicians that lasted were outlaws for real. Merle Haggard, like Owens, was a California Dust Bowl emigrant. I don't remember him appearing on *Hee Haw*, but he probably did. Haggard sang to expose discontent. He grew up in a converted old railroad car that was rattled by passing trains. Dropping out of school at fourteen, he hitch-hiked west: "For the first time there wasn't somebody hollering at me, telling me what to do. I enjoyed it. I had some certain things in my life I wanted to do. I wanted to hop a freight. I wanted to work in the oil fields. I wanted to play the guitar." His record of petty crimes mounted and at twenty he was sentenced to two years in prison. Having actually been there, Haggard doesn't romanticize the experience. He sings like he's trying to escape. Yet prison rehabilitated him; it was there he saw Johnny Cash sing and decided that music was the route to freedom.

I used to find Haggard rough to listen to. He wasn't pretty, but more like a dirt road or getting cussed out or digging a hole. The patriotic stuff, "Okie from Muskogee," "Fighting Side of Me," I heard day in and day out, on the radio and from the mouths of my relatives. These reactions against the '60s war protests upset me. How could you not want peace? How can you justify a purposeless war? My relatives and Merle Haggard insisted that we had to support the fighters and the veterans. I didn't agree with them and I still don't, but I understand now that the kids sent over were the ones without college deferments. Mostly blacks and working-class whites. The protesters came off to them like spoiled brats with free rides. So when Merle Haggard says in these songs that he's proud to be from Nowhere, and that he'll fight someone who's trashing AMERICA (in caps, the Big America), he's saying, I have value and so do my sons and friends from this podunk town who are getting shot. It wasn't some abstract patriotic pride—it was defense of everything he believed himself to be. Sacrifice matters.

What an outsider might see as schlock is real emotion if your life is slipping. Being in love or falling hard are real and surprising and can make the words in popular songs seem true. Musicians like Bob Dylan, who masks emotion with wordplay and makes us guess what he means, admit these old country singers had soul. Dylan, Elvis Costello, and most of the other balladeers of the baby-boom generation modeled their music after George Jones, Hank Williams, and Woody Guthrie (along with black blues artists), but these contemporary poet-singers are usually not confessional. We don't know if Bob Dylan has a drug problem or beats his ex-wife, while we know more than we want to know about George Jones's relationship with a bottle. We don't know much about Elvis Costello's childhood, but we know everything about Elvis Presley's. To reveal yourself is to risk being a fool. For self-conscious intellectually trained people, this can be pretty embarrassing. If you're going to be a gushy honest sap, better to be unaware that you are. As soon as you know, you're posing.

Most country musicians try to stay genuine by keeping in touch with their fans. They sign autographs, play opries and honky-tonks on their way up and down, and rarely reach the arena-sized venues of rock stars. Without everybody looking, they can be a little more themselves. Doing good work under the glare of adulation is difficult for all artists, and dangerous to the emotionally fragile. Maybe it's better to be like Merle Haggard, not wildly famous but respected. To become an icon nearly always means doom—loved too much, they lose themselves inside the heavenly gates of Graceland, victims of what they've been made to be. Crossing over to pop means losing your soul.

Country spoke of being broke and broken, of laboring in a U.S. that celebrates bagel-and-plain-cream-cheese briefcase-carrying tie-guy success. Workers are still around, although

growing up with rednecks and punks

they're in danger of losing their jobs; towns remain, although their character is disappearing. It's the same logic that says taking people off welfare rolls eliminates the need for welfare; pushing people out of farms and towns will mean that there is no more working poor. Nobody sings much about these losses. We'll put the country dancing on Gap commercials; we like country now. We'll hang a "hand-crafted" heart on our door, put a sunflower on our decorative apron. Everyone from the city wants her quiet piece of land, never mind that the farmer is gone.

If we say a music is honest, we mean that it is relatively non-commercialized. It isn't over-produced and just there to make money. It has something to say. As the music industry becomes as conglomerated as the book industry, as big business swallows up the small, it becomes harder to say anything even if you want to. In order to hear roots music, be it country or rock or bluegrass, we may have to turn away from our TVs and radios and head down to the bar where the local band is hawking their homemade CDs. The best of innovative recorded country is the "no alternative" movement: Wilco, Lucinda Williams, Iris DeMent, Ricky Skaggs and other traditionalist innovators. Storytellers and archivists, they break rules and preserve history. The Jeff Tweedies and Steve Earles and Kelly Willises give me hope, but slip between the grooves of airplay and are known mostly to the collegiate fringe. People who really live in the country can't afford to experiment on CDs by musicians who aren't on the radio. They don't have Internet MP3s or antennas that reach wide urban bands. And major record labels keep their lock on radio stations. Without rebellion, country music will disappear into clever upbeat hooks indistinguishable from A.M. "lite." And without real country music, country culture slips away as surely as small-town businesses. Like the subdivisions that spring up on the former cornfields, mainstream c&w is in the neighborhood of country, but it's a suburb just the same.

LOST CAUSE AND SIN

PINK HOUSES AND FAMILY TAVERNS: A RIDE THROUGH MELLENCAMP TOWN

I KNEW A LOT OF GUYS like John Mellencamp: physically messed-up (too scrawny, too big, too weathered, not fashionable), feisty, obstinate, occasionally mean, argumentative, macho, hurt by women, heavy drinkers, proud of where they came from, religiously superstitious true believers. Maybe Mellencamp isn't personally like that—I've never met him—but his music is, which is why just about everyone I've known from small towns played his music and recognized themselves in it.

He was everything I wanted to leave behind, every jerk relative and bully classmate. It's hard for me to find the romantic side of bar fights, cigarettes, bad jokes, and restless anger, although male country singers see it that way all the time. Sexual attraction, however, is another matter, and there's something in Mellencamp's desperate desire to be in your face that's kinda, well, sexy. As he gets older, he's more willing to lay himself out there, far more exposed than Springsteen, and in this lies guts. Courage is a turn-on for women. While we expect guys to accept our independence and reject visions of feminine wimpiness, we still want our men to be strong and certain. Plain-ass sexually tough. A guy who can go all night. That's why you can buy a poster of John Mellencamp at my favorite record store: this grizzly guy of fifty staring moodily toward a field, not the camera. *I'm damned iconographic,* he seems to be saying, and college females buy this poster and put it on their dorm walls. When I was twenty, I didn't stick mid-life hicks up on my apartment refrigerator. Only lately have we accepted our rockers as age defying—like Retin-A cream; they give us hope in their admission that they, too, are human, and that it is with age that they have learned to speak their true name.

Mellencamp's hits used to work too hard to be Guthrie-esque and rural, and so I didn't quite believe them. Mellencamp himself calls these songs "math": formula music. "When things are inspired," he told author Bill DeMain, "they're beautiful. But you know, math songs are the biggest hits in the country right now. Turn on the radio and that's all you hear is math. That shit can't be inspired." I could've cared less about "Jack and Diane"; Billy Joel told the same story a lot more inventively in "Scenes from an Italian Restaurant," the story of two lovers who marry, find themselves faced with Sears furniture, and divorce. It's the same old saw: How do we stare down the wild young studs we used to be? Springsteen rocked about it in "Glory Days," and every Bob Seger song crammed this dead-end message down our throats. Not to mention Andrew Lloyd Webber going poignant in "Memory," Barbra Streisand whining "The Way We Were," and even, if you really want to stretch it, "Big Yellow Taxi." *(You don't know what you've got 'til it's gone.)*

When Mellencamp wasn't pretending to be a hot young punk, he was waving his arms and yelling "I'm going to write a better anthem than Springsteen's!"—which to me always sounded forced, like he was trying to get over and didn't have much to say. Mellencamp, like a lot of short guys—no offense—had an inferiority complex, the kind that got him sucked in with a manager that persuaded him to name himself after a wildcat and be packaged and marketed like Axyl Rose or Boy George. The ultimate in humiliating hype was "Johnny Cougar Day," when Mellencamp and his band rode a limo through Seymour, Indiana, in 1976, cheered on by a parade, banners, and girls. This incident was covered by the rock press, which laughed. Nobody's ever let him forget it. While small towns are safe in their insularity, they're not places made for building the self-worth and savvy that keep you from getting used. There's not a lot of sophisticated business jockeying; if there were, folks wouldn't be getting laid off from the factory.

What you get, though, is work ethic. You keep at it until the job is done; you never walk away. "How do you tell the same couple of stories again and again and make it interesting? That's a challenge. It's called work," Mellencamp has said.

As soon as he could, he dropped the "Cougar" and his man-

growing up with rednecks and punks

ager, became himself, and put out a great album, *The Lonesome Jubilee,* about the people he knew in Indiana. He grew up in a small town not far from Bloomington. I grew up in a small town—or rather just outside a small town—not far from Springfield, Illinois. Here's what I think rings true in the best Mellencamp songs:

- Small towns are full of scary people, and weird things happen there.
- Small towns are full of defeated people who are being used by the system and who continue on because they don't have any choice (and like being alive).
- Violence and prejudice in small towns are as casual as a slap in the face.
- Small towns lack pretension because everyone is struggling.
- Fighting back is fun. Without defense, there is no pride.
- Heartbreak is the same everywhere.

It's the "I know I'm a hick but screw you" attitude that gets Mellencamp his obsessive, devoted following. It's the recognition that the ladder to success isn't even near your yard—but so what? It's the choice not to have a cell phone, a business deal, an advanced degree in an esoteric subject. It's the rejection of all that city people need, in what they believe makes up the good life: a fine ethnic restaurant, a cappuccino bar, a jazz club. What do they appreciate, then? The town square, a beer, a good guitar player, the woods. Home.

Students laugh when I mention Bruce Springsteen, who they see as an old show-off, but they don't laugh at Mellencamp. They write papers about him; they see him as a radical, the only defender of a way of life they may be leaving behind. "He's real," they say. What they mean by this, I think, is that he's like them. They trust him to be direct; "honest," Mellencamp said in an interview with Bob Guccione, Jr., "is better than cool." While

Springsteen used to be like us, he's since gone on to become a myth. Mellencamp's like the guy down the street, the one who can never start his junk car, who got laid off and ended up with a better job at the garage.

But he's not a loser; willing to take risks, he emerges with the unusual. Mellencamp's been credited with the revival of "roots music," the "no alternative" movement—which encompasses what critic Bill DeMain calls "garage band spirit, blue jeans and t-shirts (and) attachment to home turf." Before Wilco and Blues Traveler and Dave Matthews made it trendy, Mellencamp did it. "Look," Mellencamp has said, "I put accordion and violins and everyone laughed—now I turn on the radio and someone else is getting over on my idea." Nobody will argue that he's got a great band. He insists that the instruments and arrangements are important, that people feel the music before the words; but in his own case, he's got it wrong. Like it or not, he's a message singer. The fans see themselves as the lives in his songs.

I once did office work at a center for domestic violence. The receptionist, Karen, was a Mellencamp fanatic. She drove to work from Petersburg, forty miles away, and if she got in too early, she slept on the floor beside her desk. Her parents owned a bar in Petersburg, and she grew up tending drinks and waiting tables. Karen loved her town, and she loved *Spoon River Anthology,* in which Edgar Lee Masters tells the story of the Petersburg folk who populate the hilly rural cemetery. She knew everybody and everybody knew her, but being the daughter of a tavern owner hardly put her among the town's elite. Her tan pickup had her name inscribed beneath the door, and she liked guys but never had a serious boyfriend. Wanting nothing to do with college, she had no plans of leaving her beloved Petersburg or getting any job requiring ambition. She just wanted to have fun and drift, protected by her rowdy friends. Karen hated country music and city music; only Mellencamp had her fanatical allegiance, because he loved his town the way she loved hers. Although it's possible she read him wrong—Mellencamp speaks through characters, the people who watch their days go by.

I never liked small towns much when I actually lived there; they only look decent in the sunrise of nostalgia. I sure never thought I wanted to die in one; it was the circle drive with no exit, lined by rows of identical prefab two-story white-sided frame houses. Girls in my town would never admit, even in whispers, to wanting to be an artist, a writer, or even a teacher. Going to college seemed fraught with risk, and those who did go expected nothing beyond the A.A. or B.A. that would get them some useful job—after, of course, the kids were raised. Sitting on the steps of the Methodist church and watching the cars go by, we never shared our wildest dreams. Getting away was as distant a notion as a trip to Europe; it was something done by people on TV. So when Mellencamp sings of wanting to die in a small town—"that's good enough for me"—it sounds like giving up.

When my parents moved to that house in the country, I changed schools. From fifth grade on, I took the school bus to Rochester. My mother and aunt and uncle's graduation pictures hung in the high school cafeteria. They watched me as I ate, regaling me with their stories of cheerleading and athletic successes while my friends and I talked about books. My cousin's daughters go to that same school, and the pictures must watch them, too.

Long before I was born, my grandparents ran a restaurant in Rochester. When it burned down, they moved to that spot of land in the country. Grandma was a silent and private woman, and she hated the way everyone in that small town knew everyone else's business. She had one friend, Vivian Coffey, a round munchkin woman with a poof of black hair and butterfly-wing glasses; her style was plaids with stripes and untied white Keds with holes in the toes. Vivian roamed town, sometimes helping out at her husband Bill's service station, Coffey's Texaco up by

Highway 29. Bill, a lean, tall man as silent as Vivian was a chatterer, put me in mind of Hank Williams and so he seemed to have secret depth. Their daughter, Becky Lynn (I was, uh, Becky Jo), became my best friend. Long summer days were spent sitting on the jutting cement beneath the gas station's plate glass window, eating free ice cream bars and talking, of course, about boys. The ping-ping of the cars driving in, the farmers with their dirty caps and dirty hands, talking about troubles, the sarcastic, bitter teenagers who paid in quarters, the hiss of air filling rubber, and drills welding parts or whatever all happened out there in that garage: I loved it. The gasoline tang, the slick pools of oil that swirled like kaleidoscopes after a rain, the sound of men figuring a problem: this was the best of that town, and this is what I like to recall when I hear a Mellencamp song. Men talking crops, work, jokes, shot deer.

When we weren't riding bikes, swapping lies, and soaking in gas fumes, we hung out in Becky Coffey's backyard, a dog pen–wilderness that ran beside their frame house and extended back to the property line of the grade school. Beyond the trampled-shit area (they raised Irish setters), the weedy grass was mat for cartwheels, red rover, tag, and other games that children mostly now play in gym class. Far from supervision, we did whatever we pleased, mostly jacks and cloud-staring and the teasing cruelties that led us toward adult competitions. Without schedules for team sports, summer classes, and camp, time extended like a broken rubber band; it would disappear come fall, but for the summer we only felt it stretching in the humid Midwestern heat.

Becky's house held the allure of sloppy sensuality: empty Coke bottles and chip sacks on the floor, and her sisters' slingshot white bras and girdles draped over bed stands and lampshades, promising bosoms and voluptuousness that I would *never* have. That Becky would make excuses and tidy things in the kitchen while I stood breathing in the absolute freedom of it went right past me. That some people looked down

growing up with rednecks and punks

on them was also something I didn't comprehend; having little money myself, I felt the criticism and condescension but didn't understand it—I thought it had something to do with *me*. Even then, in the '60s, city newcomers seeking whiteness were filling the town my relatives had grown up in. These professionals made the old townies look like rubes. Mellencamp's cozy "we're all in this together, down and out in our small town" attitude was never anything I'd experienced. There was old town, and suburban, and those of us who were relics just enjoyed the sunset until it all went down.

There wasn't much else to do. Towns move at their own pace and nothing happens but that the neighbors keep their eyes on you and talk about who did what. You're pegged by money, smarts, size, strength, parents, grandparents, great-grandparents, land, house, parents' jobs; and there's no escape. Unless you cut all ties. Authority always wins; dreams go up like paper in fire; Eden burns and we're left again. In a small town, we know whose parents drink, whose screw around, whose are kindly, and whose frighten us. Anyone not white is considered dangerous. (The only black family to move to our town was driven out when someone scrawled "nigger" on their garage.) By sixth grade, our school had alcoholics, truants, and potheads, and by seventh, pregnant girls and any kind of drug you might want. Kids die in cars, slicing around figure-eight turns, because all you can do is drink, drive, drive, park, drive, avoid cops, and wipe out doing ninety-five. The good kids, so-called, like me, stayed home and watched *Monty Python* on fuzzy TV and fantasized about bohemia, sophisticated men, and getting-into-trouble. Mellencamp romanticizes that part: the cut-up, the rebel, the musician who hung out in the black clubs. That's only charming for awhile, though.

Mellencamp's later music shows the turnabout of the kid having kids. When we're small, angry, energetic, electric, people let us slide. In an artist or performer or searcher, spontaneity gets mixed up with being childlike: we're let off the hook of responsibility, we let ourselves off. Mellencamp struggles with growing up and with the need for the rest of the world to move along with him.

Will my kids laugh at me? Will I fail them? How can we be good people? The answer to the first two questions is always yes, and it is against this that Mellencamp fights. For awhile, it was enough to do it through youthful rocking: "R.O.C.K. in the U.S.A.," "Cherry Bomb,"... dancing and playing all night, letting it be known that AGE WILL NOT GET US, that being young is the affirmation of joy and bucking the system. Then Mellencamp had a heart attack. Nothing cuts off wild rebellion better than that. He still smokes, but he doesn't eat the usual country eggs-and-meat diet. We scale back, resolve conflicts, sort the laundry into separate piles and throw a lot of it away. In the liner notes for his "best of" collection, Mellencamp talks about coming to terms with his family. He tells of getting punched by his dad, turning to his grandparents for support and protection. What can you do but get pissed off? Anger makes for energy and will, but kicks back on you if you don't do something constructive with it. In the face of mortality the men in Mellencamp's family made peace. They accepted who they were.

Mellencamp's later songs struggle toward resolution. True to growing up Nazarene, they're full of apocalypse. (Indiana has its Bible Belt tendencies, like southern Illinois, where a famous landmark is a gigantic white cross perched on a hill in Bald Knob.) Will the kids make things better, the way I always thought they would? Will I be forgiven for my wilder transgressions? There will be a reckoning. We like to see adolescence as the time of lost innocence, but it's when we're middle-aged that we get slammed by the hardest realities. That's when the doors of escape close and we see that time is short. Friends and family start declining and dying from illnesses and frailties, so we stop and add up our lists. We think we can sidestep this in America, land of beginnings and rock and roll. We were raised for discovery, not responsible acceptance of fate.

With middle age comes turning over; finding a leaf on the trail, we inspect its dirty, dark underside, where earth and insects hang. What we see disturbs us, so we run for liquor, antidepressants, golf, work, divorce—all those diversions we call "mid-life crisis." Assessment and retrospection are good, but we don't stop unless we must; it takes a crisis, like Mellencamp's heart attack, to make us think. Thinking is humiliating; we're not supposed to slide back, to show our weaknesses. Who knows what will happen if people know who we really are.

Mellencamp celebrates disaster. He applauds "the full catastrophe of life"; better to live, he says, than to play too straight or lie. Lying might be easier; but to be a rebel means to go after the lively truth of the situation, kicking against resignation. Our coming deaths make us question our days, our pasts, who we have been, what we want. Guys run off and buy sports cars; women embrace lovers; we abandon jobs and places, looking for all we wanted to become. At forty, we are hit in the face with almost-relinquished dreams.

His anthems are gone. No more songs that get played over the Fourth of July fireworks. Now it's little screwed-up lives: the adulterer, the waitress, the kids moving on and away. The songs are the red-and-blue of fading bruises. Jumpin' joy catch tunes have turned into devastation love songs (*Jack and Diane went to the movies, they saw Richard Pryor screaming on his knees for his lover.... How could I have been wrong about you, how could I have been so wrong about you, with love on my side?*). Old themes of punished sinners (there's no redemption for people like you and me, babe) haunt like palpable phantoms, eternally screwed. Mellencamp's naïveté bugged the critics; he sang about forgotten people, lost farms, and thought this would open people's eyes and change their behavior. He denies this; he says that when he wrote "Scarecrow," about the end of farming, he knew things would get worse: "It's disappointing but I'm not astonished. Any time the government takes control of something like they have the farm problem, you can about bet it's not gonna go in the way of the common person."

It's a hopeless fight against impossible circumstances. When Mellencamp sang about America as the land of little pink houses for all, he was laughing, but meant it; a house is permanence, the step past survival—it beats the hell out of a trailer. It means mortgages and wives/husbands and kids and dogs. For awhile, Mellencamp embraced the fantasies that built random people into community; but then it struck him that it didn't work. The factory goes under, and the pink house becomes a burden. Wives leave, parents die, kids ridicule. There's nothing to rebel against but yourself. Life is frightening, nothing lasts forever, life is hard.

In his middle age Mellencamp finds confidence, titling a CD with only his name, as if it's his first; singing about self-acceptance and grabbing the moment ("Your Life Is Now," "I'm Not Running Anymore"); it's not his best album, but it's hopeful in an almost terrified adult way. His later music, full of doom, embraces the realization that we are going to hell; we can hope for the kids to save us ("Check It Out"), but, sinners all, we're out of luck. We'd better do something fast.

Rough Harvest, done to finish up his contract with Mercury Records (it's stamped "SOLD," and "PAID IN FULL"), is filled with scaled-back versions of his own and others' songs. He covers a Dylan number and his own best songs with scratchy-voiced depth. Sure, I know it exists to fulfill a contract, but it's great to hear Mellencamp singing folkie-style with harmonic vocal accompaniment and a violin—excuse me, a *fiddle.* He doesn't have to work hard to please us—he's out to please himself—and this gives the songs a surprising emotional unveiling. Line him up behind Dylan, Tim Hardin, Woody Guthrie, and even George Jones; in no way is this a pop record. Mellencamp ain't a kid.

But the kids still love him and they're right: Mellencamp calls it as he sees it. He stopped being pretentious. Like most Midwesterners, he's self-deprecating. We're all fated to being embarrassed about failed farms and "playing in Peoria." Mellencamp can't allow himself too many proclamations, because his friends will laugh. So he's macho and modest, tossing off pain because people out here are stoic. It's plain talk.

Underneath the rocking band is a plea that things be made better—and fast. The songs are as urgent as the man laid off from his factory job, the woman forced to work nights while trying to raise three kids. He tells the stories that most people don't want to hear, with the stubborn joy of someone who gets up after the punch, just to prove he can. It's music that comes out of a place where change may mean the end of a life and a way of living. Like a heartbeat, they come to their ends.

WOMEN
AMONG
PIGS

Some are mathematicians
Some are carpenter's wives.
Don't know how it all got started,
I don't know what they're doin' with their lives. . . .

—BOB DYLAN, "Tangled Up in Blue"

IN RURAL ILLINOIS, men were farmers and women became farmers' wives. Or they chose not to be farmers' wives, instead becoming carpenters' wives or welders' wives or crewmen's wives. Being a farmer's wife was not for the faint-hearted, since it meant that, above all wifely roles, there would be no escape. The land was the land and it definitely was not going anyplace. Or so it seemed at the time.

One of the biggest farms near us was owned by a family known collectively as "the Messermachers." Their corn covered rural plots right up to the pitted road, and their pigs' aroma wafted for miles, settling over our yard. My mom once went steady with "one of the Messermacher boys" and speculated about what her life would've been as a farm wife. *A hell of a lot better,* she figured, sighing, "I went out with a *Messermacher.*" One slow afternoon we looked at photographs of a square-jawed, muscular man standing on a boulder, surrounded by gray sky. (Everything then was in black and white.) When we turned the page of her red scrapbook, the boy stretched in his basketball uniform, holding a ball soon cast to the ceiling. "I was a *cheerleader,*" Mom said, bitter over all that lost popularity. A totally different ring than "I am a housewife with a crazy husband and two weird kids stuck in the middle of nowhere with nothing to do." Had the genes been shifted, I could've been a farmer's daughter, a life with its pieces in place.

149

A Messermacher was in my class at school. Like Goofy, he was big, dumb, likable, unremarkable in every way. In a different time and place, he would've become a frat boy at the state college, then taken a job as, say, an insurance clerk or a hardware salesman. Instead, he stayed on the farm, got married, and built a fine log cabin surrounded by oak trees and brush timber. As far as I know, he's still there, and so is the farm.

In her pictures, posing with her boyfriend, Mom looks strong and bright and hopeful. In your face with optimism. She chose my dad because he was a soldier who grew up far from Illinois; she knew him through letters they exchanged during the Korean war. She wrote to many soldiers, and John Wesley was the one she picked. But letters present only one side of who we are—what we say we feel in writing doesn't always have much to do with the way we behave. Whether showing the best or the worst of us, written words hold far more sway than talk—and Mom read it all wrong. She gave up the local boy and the farm for a life of adventure. She blew that pop stand and headed for desert and pampas grass where not a single stalk of corn took root. She and Dad and Uncle Ronnie set up house until Ronnie died and Dad went wacko, and after ten years in Phoenix she ended up right back on her parents' property, under her father's thumb, a half-mile from her old high school sweetheart. Without money or even much land.

Lost chances are even more haunting when they live right down the dusty road.

My old friend from Roby, Sharmina (named for a brand of toilet paper), married a farmer. His name was Bob, I think, though it might've been Jeff or Jim or Joe. A big strapping German blond, he was as dense as a two-by-four and about as interesting. Okay, this is unfair. All I know was that he was your standard issue good ol' boy who swapped jokes with Uncle Wade, never read books or magazines or newspapers, and had

growing up with rednecks and punks

no particular hobbies like hang gliding, truck racing, or minia-ture-train building. What Bob knew was pork.

With Sharmina on his lap, he talked pigs. Sharmi looked like a sturdy beech stick, freckled and a little sunburned. Her dyed hair was an eggplant shade that on a punker would have been a declaration of independence. On Sharmi, it was a mistake of timing. The way she and her sister sat on their boyfriends' laps had something of the dirty joke in it, even though they perched rather primly. Maybe it was the way the guys held them tightly around their waists, staking claim on the women who would become their wives. By the time Sharmina was sixteen, bike rides and giggles had given way to *Bride* and *House Beautiful.*

"Don't you *love* this gown?" she once asked, opening the magazine to a sweetly smiling Norwegian with a bouquet of baby's breath. We sat cross-legged on her double bed, surrounded by ruffled yellow curtains and smiling bears and a ballerina on a stand, toe pointed, face blank. One of Sharmi's eyes, the lazy one, drifted toward the window while the other looked hard at my face. Please tell me this is the right choice, the eye stared, and I could only nod. I didn't know enough to say otherwise.

I had not for a micro-second imagined myself in the pages of *Bride* magazine. Or even thought of buying *Bride* magazine. I was leery of that lap-sitting, and that agreeable, dutiful, white-gown-and-apron thing. My mom had gotten all those dreams fulfilled and look where it got her. As I listened to Sharmina, who seemed so sure, I wondered about myself. Though I adored her cousin, who broke horses, and Jimmy Deem, the cute short guy from school, and Bob Dylan, who I was sure I'd eventually meet, I wasn't about to *do* anything. My daydreams were more com-prehensible than that awkward, hot-and-nervous-squirmy-ac-quiescent stuff that went with guys. Where was the chivalry? The earth-rocking epiphany? The obsession and beauty? Still, it had to be me, some problem with me.

Sharmina grasped her boyfriend the way you'd hug the edge

of a shallow pool. Bob became the check, her life's routine. She wore her eyeliner thick and her blusher heavy, because she thought this was what men liked. Her eyebrows were plucked into arches and her hair was curled high, and she rubbed her skin with lemons to fade her freckles.

"He won't like me in the mornings." She popped open a can of Pepsi as she paced the kitchen. The sliding glass door looked out upon the fields, and, far past, my aunt and uncle's house. A shaggy white mutt, Toya, barked at a squirrel chattering from a huge oak. "How can I keep my makeup from getting smeared when I sleep?" She used to talk of Europe and horses and painting. Of mistakes, fooling-around troubles, why being a girl was humiliating. Of covering up, putting on a face—she thought I didn't act enough, that I was as transparent as cellophane. Now she looked steadfastly ahead at the territory of Bob, and I couldn't tell if she felt for him, or if this was her most clever disguise. Was this what growing up was all about?

It wasn't that I didn't like Bob—he was simply amorphous, the white farmhouse in the center of the field. Plain, basic, with a storm cellar. The only time I heard him talk much was with my uncle. He and Wade joked in that way of country guys—work and sex the compass points—and while sex was often laughed at, work never was. Their currency was the farm's fortune and the tavern's joke. The clap on the back, the mumbled secret, the loud guffaw. Bob looked abashed and rather pleased when he emerged from Wade's backslaps, initiated into the realm of Patton men. Sharmina's father, David, was Wade's brother. Though they lived next door, Wade and David never spoke—yet Sharmi was still the niece, and this made Bob one of the family. I felt a little sorry for him!

I tried to adjust to my best country friend's leap into adulthood—the kind of adulthood that I hoped to avoid. Marriages kill friendships, and no matter what a person does to try to salvage old connections, they pull apart. Marriage builds couple links, joined rings; a single female or male creates a triangle.

growing up with rednecks and punks

Somebody's jealous or threatened. Pairs merge, and we almost forget who we used to be.

Our last chat in her girlhood bedroom was about decoration.

"It's going to be so nice having a whole house to myself." We sat on her bed, an array of magazines on the blanket between us. Instead of *True Confessions* and *Tiger Beat,* they were *Better Homes and Gardens* and *House Beautiful.* She clasped her stuffed dog, red fingernails pressed into fake fur. In her sunshiny room, with its bedspread with frills, a framed sketch of a galloping horse, a dining room chair in the corner, round throw rug in braided circles covered with dog hair—these temporary bedrooms of children—we felt our own departures. A month after graduating high school, she'd be walking down the aisle.

I never thought to ask if she loved Bob. I kind of assumed she didn't. It just didn't feel like that. Bob was an inevitability. In all our talks of sex, of *Modern Romance,* she never spoke of kissing Bob. Her eyes shone over the notion of the wedding gown, but not when she said Bob's name. That stray eye always looked someplace else, but it wasn't moving.

I visited Sharmina's new home only once. I was with my mother, but I don't remember why. It was a visit with a purpose, to buy a dog or sheep or a butchered pig or maybe eggs. Calling Sharmi to talk like old times would've been awkward. I would have lost my words.

Bob met us at the car and showed us around the yard. The two-story farmhouse was penned on three sides by corn. Bob's drawl was warm as he took us to the chicken run and the pig pens, each footstep falling on family property. Bob *was* that farm. He didn't have much of interest to tell us, but that didn't matter because language doesn't count for much on a farm. Words don't do the work. He moved as slowly as a steer, in a way that fit the rhythms around him. A hot, sleepy pace. His voice was soft, even loving, as he talked of his animals. Soon his children would help him work that land. They would speak only to one another—no co-workers, no bosses, no staff. The expectation of inheritance was as real as the well cistern, the tractor, the fence. The finality of the farm, his future, his family's future, existed in direct opposition to my own flux. I ran my hand along the rough post of the chicken pen, along the slick wire, jealous that he never had to question whether this place was right, because it was the only place. I understood now why Sharmina was drawn to Bob's steadiness, why she would want to have her feet on this ground.

And where was Sharmi on this tour? In the house, of course, where I will always envision her.

Already there was a baby, a daughter in a room yellower than daffodils. On a single shelf covered with toys perched a homemade, malformed Snoopy dog, doing (or trying to do) the happy foot-flinging Snoopy dance. The menagerie of pastel pets looked not huggable but hard, despite their wistful thread smiles. The room was in-progress, wallpaper stopping in the center of a wall, neon plastic cubicles waiting for when the child would want more. I tried not to look at the infant wrapped in her dotted blanket, on her stomach, face turned in that unaware, translucent way of sleeping children. I wanted a baby, I wanted this life, and knew I couldn't tolerate it—but it didn't stop the yearning, the desire to hold a small human. I missed my younger cousins, I missed being with kids. Sadness surged in some hormonal sweep and I got out of the room.

Though the baby slept, Sharmina went no farther than earshot, bound by that maternal cord. She had that blowzy vague face of mothers of young children, run ragged with distraction, sleeplessness, edging between bliss and madness. Already she was pregnant with her second.

I don't know if she was glad to see me. She liked to look nice and she didn't even have on lipstick, and her red-dyed hair had turned into what she called a mousy brown, and instead of ratted into country "big hair" it hung straight around her face in a bad British shag. "I'm sorry to be a mess," she kept apologizing,

growing up with rednecks and punks

patting her face; she seemed two degrees faded, like a vibrant shirt left too long to dry in the sun. Sharmina had become a moth with folded wings; you almost wonder if it's still alive.

"This is the dining room." Like most Midwestern houses, this space was used for company; it held an oak table surrounded by heavy chairs (probably passed down from a grandma), a china cabinet with flimsy doors (the kind you'd get at a mid-price chain furniture store), a woven rug on a hardwood floor, and windows looking out upon corn. The room was shadowy, a place to walk through between kitchen and living room TV. What distinguished it were the walls. A luminescent midnight blue, the effect was an attempted cheerfulness twisted to twilight darkness. From the salmon pink living room to the half-painted purple kitchen, the rooms existed like separately wrapped gift boxes, happy and forced. Along the ceiling, borders were finished and borders begun—hearts and fleurs-de-lis. "I designed it myself," she said, and didn't sound exactly proud. "I went a little too far. I keep trying to adjust." On the dining room wall was the framed pencil sketch of a galloping horse that she'd drawn when I first knew her—its mane flying back against a landscape of white paper.

I praised and reassured, faced with her pinched and worried self-consciousness. Even expected visitors can be a disruption when the only folks you see are relatives. Suddenly there you are, standing in the outsider's light, seeing it all as they must, knowing you have been revealed. At the door, as my mother waited beside the car, Sharmina put a hand on my shoulder. "Don't do this."

I just looked at her. Something familiar in it frightened me. The darkness despite the bright day, the silence of sleep, the baskets of laundry; . . . add a soap opera, it could've been my mom.

"This is harder than I thought," she whispered. "I wish I'd seen some of the world."

"All I'm seeing is the community college," I said, "it's not so

WOMEN AMONG PIGS

pretty," pulled between wanting land and child and needing to get out of the house and go on a fast drive. What countered in her green eyes was this: college *was* a world.

"Don't settle for the first."

I wasn't about to settle at all, but Sharmi wasn't talking to me. She was seeing herself at sixteen, riding her bike anywhere she wanted, all summer long.

She let go my arm and we promised to see each other soon. We traded phone numbers and hugged. She was inches taller than me and firm and tough as anything. I don't think she wanted to let go. But I sure did. When I stepped into the glaring August light, stumbling as my eyes tried to adjust, she stayed in so that she might hear the baby cry.

That was the last time I saw her. As far as I know, she's still standing behind the screen door.

A year or so after seeing Sharmi, I got involved with a farmer. Well, he tried to be a farmer—what he really was was a farmer's son.

Fletcher Doberman was one of the few English graduate students in the small quirky college that I went to in Springfield, Illinois. Then known as Sangamon State, the school attracted radicals and artists who liked its enclave-ish privacy and proximity to an enormous governmental bureaucracy. (Springfield, I once heard, was second only to Washington, D.C., in its load of officials and official paper.) The school had spun off two sizable Communistic communes, a bevy of Marxists, a slew of community activists, and a nest of artists. Fletch was a poet—my first.

His elegant, gentleman-farmer lyrics eschewed capital letters. Filled with aquamarine bottles and green plants, the poems had no action. Still lifes, their emotional changes were so subtle as to be nearly nonexistent. He had feelings though, I think.

It wasn't love at first sight, and my liking swung between the affection of a cousin and a speculative hope for evolution. I was recovering from addiction to a jazz musician, and Fletcher was as good as methadone—respectable, placid, and sweet in a dismissive kind of way. Model-gorgeous, he had a blond furry chest and perfect white teeth. Along with his farmland, he owned a degree in engineering from the University of Illinois (for which he'd used a mind tuned to precision), and he had money to blow. He drove the only BMW in which I've ever ridden, a morning-sky blue kept parked on the far edge of the university lot. Not a scrap of paper or a dented pop can marred the carpeted floor of *this* baby. He tossed around cash like confetti, though he made little effort to wine and dine me. I was too easy—ten years younger, never out of jeans, cursing like a tart, demanding nothing but polite attention. So poor that going to a mid-scale restaurant was a big deal. The making-out was lackadaisical—he was a peculiarly passionless guy for a poet, at least with me. I sometimes wondered if he was gay, with his picky tidiness and attention to his own good looks. Yet he married at least three times after he knew me: a cocaine-addicted farm girl, a newscaster, and a reporter.

At thirty, Fletcher was dabbling in writing, but his duty was to take over the family farm. He talked little of it. His folks owned one of the largest spreads north of Springfield and he kept this identity cocooned around him like a tight wool coat. He still lived there with his parents.

I went to the farm once. The drive wound among overhanging maples and across bridges spanning the Sangamon and its creeks. When the trees cleared, the land became agriculture. The random towns were so tiny that most didn't even have a gas station—although they did have diners and maybe a bowling alley. Irrigation machines stretched across fields like water-walking bugs. This route lacked the lushness of the river bottoms, was brittle with corn stalks drying in the summer heat. While Tennessee ramblers settled my family's part of Illinois, this was hardworking, staunch Swede territory—austere, particular, and light on taverns.

After taking some of the corners that can be so confusing—

WOMEN AMONG PIGS

no road signs, no reference points but a sign for a Lutheran church—we arrived at Fletcher's farm. The usual two-story farmhouse sat amidst fields that extended as far as I could see. All of this would soon belong to Fletch; no other houses or sons were in sight.

He had work to do. Heading toward the livestock, he announced, "I hate pigs." Fletcher was a strict vegetarian, but as we leaned on the rails of the hog pen, he looked like he'd like to fry them. "When I take this place over, I'm getting rid of the damn things."

"But I thought they were intelligent—"

"Not that I can tell. They fight each other. They're hogs."

I perched on the rail while he carted buckets of grain, tossing the feed into troughs. The pigs shoved and nosed each other out of the way, fat pale things snorting and stumbling. The smell was pretty bad, although such things didn't bother me; I had spent a childhood cleaning chicken pens. What disturbed me was the pigs' fleshy pinkness; their vulnerability made me feel unprotected. I could not help but think of the ease with which they changed from living beast to bacon. So I shifted from looking at porkers to looking at Fletcher, muscles pulling against his t-shirt as he raised the buckets, white hair against brown arms. I'd never thought of him as strong, but he was. I suddenly wanted him—not just to fulfill desire, but maybe as a partner, I was so swept with wonder. Maybe I just hadn't seen him before.

As he showed me around, Fletch became downright animated. He laughed, walked slower and looser, even let his hair get messed up—and I saw him as a boy, alone except for the animals and maybe a silent father, working before and after school. And to fill the time, dreams: pictures, words, flamboyant women, and cities—everything that wasn't lonely. The sky and ground and corn made such a compact box, and he surely was at ease in it; but once you opened the lid, it was hard to pull it shut. In the meantime, you hauled grain and harvested, carrying so much load that work nearly became pleasure, became so much a part of you that you could almost forget the road.

Telling me of all he did on the farm and of all that had to be done, Fletcher became downright loquacious. Here, finally, was the subject he knew—it wasn't James Joyce, Ezra Pound, or mathematics, but feed and seed and root development. Rigid and particular at college, quiet except for the occasional slipped-in joke, formal and status-conscious, Fletcher suddenly looked happy. After all, nobody was around to see him and who was I? My folks only owned an acre. Free of its precision styling, I saw that his hair was wiry and stood from his forehead in a poignant way; I took his hand as we walked the perimeter of the corn. Cows stared at us from an adjoining property. Starlings and red-winged blackbirds fluttered randomly, and then many blackbirds rose at once from the center of the field, gliding up and then swooping down further away. A wren sang a frail melody as evening closed in. Another wren matched its call, and these were joined by more.

That night, we sat in the kitchen talking about poetry and people we knew. His parents were gone. The house was silent: no television creating background chatter, no soothing radio, not even a barking dog. We ate fresh strawberries and plain yogurt with honey—me, the fast-food maven—and sliced apples. The kitchen had the best of everything, yet its gingham curtains and wooden table made it seem cozy and old. Because it was sweet to talk with him this way, it seemed more all right to climb the stairs and make love in his boyhood bed. But never *entirely* right. Ghosts and possible disruption disturbed me. I couldn't stop my mind from running circles, even while he snored. The place felt dead. Or hollow. All was in order, but something was missing from the center. I couldn't say.

Morning was a splitting bright reality and I had a headache and an itch of guilt; we were a fraction off the mark of love and always would be. When I saw Fletcher catch his reflection in the hallway mirror and greet it with welcome, I remembered why, although the fault was also my own, with my bluntness and my stupid coltish awkwardness.

That was okay. Didn't mean we couldn't enjoy our time. After a civilized breakfast of cooked oats and skim milk, I got to ride the tractor.

Naïve as I was, I thought a tractor was a beat-up rattly jalopy with the metal seat about to fall off—the kind my uncle owned. I didn't expect to climb steps to the cab of a fully air-conditioned, damn-near-coasting machine with a stereo tape player and cushioned seats.

High up, we rumbled into the endless field, surveying it all. This farming was nothing like the kind I'd done, tugging green beans off damp stalks or pushing a hole into hard earth, sprinkling the seeds, and tamping the dirt down flat. We were so high above, so laid back listening to Peter Gabriel that we could've been in a living room. Fletcher kept glancing at me proudly. I was impressed, but troubled. This didn't fit my transcendental, Thoreauvian notions of being in touch with the land. I couldn't smell the vegetation, feel the dirt beneath my hands or its give under my shoes—there was no weather, no sweat, no spindly spiders and pushy beetles. I was shut off in the cold. Enveloped by sky and metal, surrounded by monotonous green, what I wanted more than anything was to run.

We stopped going out not long after. We stayed friends, and somewhere between marriage two and marriage three he inherited the farm and lost it. Drowned in a failure of debt. He still had the BMW, though. Maybe he owned it outright.

When I asked him about the loss, he didn't seem upset. He was as flatly soft-spoken as ever, though he wouldn't meet my eyes. I wondered if he was relieved. He didn't have to be torn between those worlds of country and city; freed from physical labor and accounting, he could move into the logorhythms of word choice. Still, he had to be missing the cows. "Cows are sweet

growing up with rednecks and punks

souls," he said that day on the farm. "Patient, agreeable. Spiritual, almost. You shouldn't eat beef. I've seen how they're butchered. They don't deserve that kind of death." Like a cow, Fletcher took what came, and he settled happily into marriage with a carrot-haired reporter. They had a shy daughter and moved away to Seattle.

I wonder how his parents felt when the land was sold, the modern machinery auctioned, the children scattered. I'm sure it wasn't what they'd pictured when they were the most prosperous farm in the county. I don't know what happened to those good staunch faces in the living room photographs. Did the parents move to a retirement condo? Did the younger sister marry well? Did anyone in town miss the Dobermans? Maybe they were all as placid as Fletch the day he looked out over the field, leaning against the hog fence, smiling the way someone does when they forget they're being watched and forget to imagine themselves. Maybe, driving the Pacific highways, Fletcher imagines corn and congratulates himself on his close escape. After all, he'd already said goodbye and a BMW is the same no matter what state you're in.

Sometimes I wonder, recalling when we walked the field hand-in-hand, if I could have stayed; accepted quiet; kept the house; helped with planting. On that farm we recognized one another, and this could have been drawn on, nurtured, might have someday yielded fruit. He could have let go of rigid ambition; I could have grown responsible. I could've supported Fletcher through the hard times, encouraged frugal commitment. *Sell the BMW,* I could've said; *buy a Chevy pickup. Take the hair gel money and put it in a savings account. Become a farming poet, not an editor. How do you prepare pig slop, honey? Here, let me help.* I could be there now, in the middle of nowhere, small in the field. Watching the blackbirds swoop up, swoop down. Like my mom, like Sharmina, I had the chance to become a farmer's wife. But I wasn't called for that. I'm too lazy to work that hard, to carry that much weight. The sky alone would have crushed me.

WOMEN AMONG PIGS

DANCING
LINES
AND
SQUARES

I KNOW HOW TO SQUARE DANCE. Not one of those stage performances where women wear matching gingham skirts and the gray-haired men their vests. I mean square dancing that's for real, a hoedown, a shindig, a party with whoops and hollers. I haven't done it since I was a kid, because as the old people die, there's nobody left to call and fiddle in a way that's in the blood, handed down, not thought through. Sure, college-educated folkies still get together in an effort to preserve a lost heritage, but country people just laugh at that kind of thing. Most true hicks have accepted the changes and have moved on to decorous line dancing to a scripted Faith Hill score. Nobody I know country square dances now. The only ones left are urban seniors trying to find dates and intellectuals who stick to the English version. It's no longer a real part of real lives, like picking strawberries or planting radishes or constructing buildings or digging mines or paying bills.

Illinois is half hillbilly, even while the redneck population decreases with every layoff-and-migration. Although we tend to think of the South as, well, south, the Mason-Dixon line creates an invisible border across the center of Illinois, and I lived just a little south of center. While in Chicago and environs they play jazz, blues, and rock (all black-influenced music), and the people don't say ain't, and they know all about latte, in the towns beneath Bloomington and going on into the rolling-bluff area that merges with Kentucky, you'll find country music (the anthems of working-class whites), considerable random "cussin'," and farm supply stores. (This isn't to say that everyone below Chicago shops at Farm and Fleet and wears overalls. Like everywhere, there are ex-hippies and college professors and artists and Marxists and transplanted toe-the-line government employees. But most people, the working-class descendents of the original Scotch-Irish and German settlers, have their roots in country.)

In the lonely hill twang of old country music is my grandma boiling fruits for jam, my uncle cursing his aching back and beating the hell out of my cousin with a tree switch, and a dog dubbed Mousy following our bikes down the gravel road; another cousin picking out a song by ear on an acoustic guitar, a red-haired freckled friend smuggling *True Confessions* to read beneath the river bridge, the worms and pottery and arrowheads surfacing when we dug with our Tonka scoops; sweet tea as we sat on metal chairs that rested on the cement slab that served as a deck, fishing for cat(fish), hanging them headless onto a tree, and scaling them, frying them up in a family festival of smoking grill and ketchup. Our music was in the lilt of speech that to urbanites just sounds uneducated, with those dropped g's and backwards words, the double negatives that meant we said no to everything and to nothing. We defined the boundaries of our lives and cut ourselves off from people outside of our own circle, the way people do when they know they don't fit into the mainstream and are mostly glad.

From Springfield down to the Ohio River, most country people come from mining stock, or are laborers or craftsmen like my family, or are (more predictably) farmers. Entire neighborhoods are balanced upon dead mine shafts that, over time, destroy foundations. Most of the mines are long unproductive. The sons of miners work on city roads, drive trucks, build houses; the daughters, if they have jobs, babysit and ring cash registers. The rest are on welfare.

To remember where they came from, people used to play music. When I was a kid, a bunch of (usually) men would throw together a string band. There'd be a drummer who was always a couple seconds off beat. A teenager might play rhythm guitar (acoustic, of course), while a man young or old but always weathered played lead. This man would be the quiet, knowing, inscrutable sort with a teetering marriage and some illegitimate children. There might be a mandolin player, a cagey smiling man or woman who seemed to tote around sly inbred mountain wisdom. But the fiddler was the center, the artist, wild and nearly deranged, able to weep and fly upon demand.

growing up with rednecks and punks

Living in the Land of Lincoln, I was lucky to have a foot in country and a toe in city. My cousins were more backwoods than I, because they went to a smaller school among the Appalachian generations, in rural Christian County. My family lived half a gas tank north, enough to mingle us among Springfield kids who would change our perceptions. My cousins' family branched extensions along the winding isolated back roads, among cabins and frame houses and trailer parks, making an intricate system of second and third cousins and aunts and all of their friends. Because they were carpenters during the housing boom, my uncle and his brother had money. Uncle Wade drove a Cadillac and flashed hundred-dollar bills and bought a pool table that dominated their living room. A successful business in a dirt-poor area, Patton Brothers pushed their good fortune into their neighbors' faces. Wade bought the general store in Roby (pop. 50), razed it, and built the showiest house around with a sunken living room and—count 'em—four bedrooms (modest by suburban standards) on a main road (a branch highway that is a blacktop two-lane). Then Patton Brothers threw their spare cash together and tossed the square dances at the Edinburg VFW Hall.

Anyone from a Midwestern town knows the importance of the VFW. The long metal buildings that look like airplane hangars are used for wedding receptions, like my cousin Brenda's, or for church chili fundraisers, or for presenting awards for patriotic essays, like the one granted my stepdaughter Monica for writing about the military sacrifices of an uncle she met only once. (It was, she said, "pure bullshit," but it brought her a thousand dollars and a trip to Cincinnati.) When food's involved, rectangular tables are set end-to-end, creating a line of denim, polyester, jello salad, and beer cups. Much like in a school cafeteria, the tables are only good for food fights and promoting clusters of people who stare down the table's length at other groups of people, creating a yin-and-yang of community bonding and divisive hostility. Everyone jockeys for attention, enjoy-

DANCING LINES AND SQUARES

ing strife and sexual adventures and a real sense of community, with a family's bonds and irritability.

Dances at the VFW are cause for realignments. The tables are folded and stacked, creating a mountain for kids. Chairs line three walls, leaving a gap for the kitchen, where liquor is served. The band, stageless, just sets up on the floor.

Leading my uncle's dances was the fiddler, a short and frail man of indeterminate oldness (in the country, forty can be pretty old if you've spent a life doing day labor), with round wire glasses and crumpled-paper skin; he also served as the caller doubling as banjo-picker. My cousin's cousin, an arrogant kid named Tom who I had a crush on and couldn't stand, played guitar with the adults, two of whom were in "real" country bands that strummed at taverns. This pair, brothers Ben and Stan, had slicked-back hair under cowboy hats, red shirts, black pants, belts with big buckles: the Western Wear look. In the country, men didn't go formal in suits; they put on their best hat and shined up their cowboy boots. The women wore pastel shirt-waist dresses or mushroom-shaped skirts; low-cut blouses or high-cut hems were considered the trademark garb of whores. (That and ratted bottle-red hair.) Pink lipstick from Avon was very okay, though. Jewelry was silver-plated with turquoise in-sets or elaborate rings with stones marking each child's birth date; or, for men, simple string ties, some with bolos of phoe-nixes. Earrings were clip-on baubles, never dangly. Decoration came in embroidery on shirts and stitchery on boots: firebirds, floral swirls, lightning bolts. Among kids, jeans (and hats for boys or "big hair" for girls) and tucked-in plaid snap-button shirts; the jeans were forced into boots, because what was the point of owning a hundred-dollar pair of shoes if nobody saw them?

The dances were a holdover from front-porch get-togethers, except now the community was scattered, driving from all over Christian County. There seemed to me, as a twelve-year-old, an

growing up with rednecks **and** punks

air of forced fun, a desperate need for these dances to come off. If they didn't (went the mumbled fear), no one would have them again. At the poker table, my uncle and aunt worried about how there was no place for people to "blow off," no good drinking spot that wasn't a dirty rat hole like the bar in Buckhart (a town that was a tavern surrounded by five houses and five satellite dishes), nowhere to kick back, take the kids, see the neighbors. The square dances were a last effort to grasp the old ways that were falling like bulldozed trees.

I tried to fit in at the dances, but never could. I was already too much the outsider. Maybe I read too much, did too much thinking. Maybe it was because I'd lived the first eight years of my life in a city. What I did was watch, ankles crossed, a dork in the homemade skirt my mother made me wear, wishing I had a boyfriend and could two-step.

To kill time, I played games to entertain my young cousins or cracked jokes with Grandma. She would never dance. Just sat there smoking a Kool and downing a screwdriver, her gray hair swept up into a French twist. "So, how's the Kool-Aid treatin' ya?" she'd say, or "Surely you're not saying you won't do-si-do?" with a secretive smile. Though her early years were spent in Prohibition-era Chicago, she never flat-out said, "Having fun hanging out with these idiot rubes getting shit-faced and showing off?" but this was implied by her crackling grin. When Grandpa finally pulled me up to take part in the Virginia Reel, he would prompt me with, "Now, you don't want to be a slug, do ya? You're missing it!" They worried over my tendency to stick my nose in a book and my head under the covers.

I thought I hated to dance, but once I got up there I felt special. You know how it is: "no, no, I don't want to look dumb, but well, okay, if you say so" and then once you're out there you find great joy in the whirling and the rushing and the show of it all. Grandpa was an expert dancer, graceful and precise. Maybe you don't know how a square dance works—something I find hard to imagine, but that I know is likely. The dance I liked best wasn't square. In a reel, two lines of people face each other, each partner across from the other. Like a zipper, the connection's made with the opposite, while every piece relies upon the other to create a workable whole. So where does the square come in? Most of our dances, except for the Virginia Reel, were arranged in open blocks, with the partner changing as the dance went on. They got quite elaborate, especially since the caller would improvise to make things more exciting. The dances themselves are far older than our country. England and France traded square dance techniques for hundreds of years, and America tossed in the Irish jig and the improvisational call. The Midwestern version differs from Western square dancing in that it involves considerable stepping and gets raucous, while Western dancing (the kind taught in grade school) is smoother, sliding. The dance as it's performed for audiences is far more controlled and sedate than the ones I swung around in. Most performance dances rely upon recordings, which eliminate spontaneity, unpredictability, emotion, and the sync that musicians and callers fall into with their dancers. The form that evolved out of Appalachia, with a couple "visiting" from square to square and then lining up for reels, is mostly adapted for performance so that all couples move all the time. And that matching costume thing—my family never did that, although there were some old folks who did.

Our dances were driven by hill music, never standard Top-40 Nashville. Alan Lomax, a big-city idealist, documented the folk music of whites and blacks in the 1950s. Lomax said that hillbilly music "give(s) the listener a feeling of security, for it symbolizes the place where he was born, his earliest childhood satisfactions, his religious experience, his pleasure in community doings, his courtship and his work." It expresses joy and grief in its embrace of the happy moment (through dance and the music's emphasis on drink and love and home) and the acknowledgment that people die and nothing lasts. Mike Seeger

growing up with rednecks **and** punks

defines hillbilly music as a conglomeration of "old unaccompanied English ballads like 'Barbara Allen,' new American songs like 'Wild Bill Jones,' old fiddle tunes like 'Devil's Dream,' and newer banjo tunes like 'Cumberland Gap.' It's a rich and varied heritage of music—as rich as the roots music of any country."

The kind I heard mixed the old chestnuts à la Bill Monroe with ancestral ballads; then, during breaks in the dancing, with classic country-western (Hank Williams, Loretta Lynn). The heart of this Americana twang comes from fiddling, a way of playing the violin that was brought over from Germany, Scotland, and Ireland and developed in the isolated pockets of the Appalachian hills. Old-time fiddling emerged from the joining of banjo and violin styles after the Civil War, and was introduced to the area through traveling black minstrel shows. It was in Appalachia that blues and gospel came across the European fiddling tradition. Appalachian fiddle music carries the keening of the bagpipe and follows the melodic line in a way that most bluegrass fiddle music doesn't.

The fiddler was the community sage and the final carrier of the heritage, who knew the words and melodies that passed through generations and that would likely die out with the next. Even when I was young, families no longer sat on porches playing music. We kids were ashamed of the old ways, and played songs from the Top-40 reprints in music books, or by ear from the radio. Most of us had no access to the keeper of the old stories. The fiddler got his chance to be heard only at the dances.

Fiddlers don't tend to talk much. This is why the recorded history of the people and this music is skimpy. A Brown University professor conducted one of the few interviews with a rural fiddler in 1990. Ethnomusicologist Jeff Titon talked with Clyde Davenport, a Kentuckian of little schooling who made his own instruments and played at people's houses, and saw his ability as mystical, something not to be questioned—"a gift," not a talent. He didn't play for money, because there wasn't much; he played because it was who he was. As a young father Clyde moved to Indiana to work in a Chrysler factory; Indiana, like southern Illinois, is full of migrated Appalachians seeking opportunity. In time, he and his wife moved back to Kentucky, where Clyde worked as a janitor. Jobs like this don't affect a worker's community standing. When there aren't jobs to be had, nearly everyone is broke (except for the outsiders who run things), and any job beats welfare. Social distinctions come out of ancestry and habits: people who keep a lot of junk cars, who sleep around (too obviously), or are "snooty" or "different" tend to be outcasts. Clyde fiddled for fun and for his neighbors, and never tried to show off by becoming a professional touring musician. Because of this, he was able to keep the old songs, not becoming slickly bluegrass or c&w or otherwise commercializing himself and losing the folkways. He owns many homemade fiddles, and prefers a "medium-toned fiddle," one that's not "coarse-toned" or "rough" or "keen and high." "Medium's just right," Clyde told Jeff.

Our fiddler, a slight man, had everyone's deference. He was aged, emulated, and assumed wise. He tapped the rhythm with his shoe and his voice was a rusty bark. Before the manic dancing, he set a mood with melancholy. The fiddle, a worn honey-brown, cried the "Tennessee Waltz," a weepy tale of lost love. Two old couples danced while people my parents' age sat in folding chairs looking stunned. The loud talk dissipated to a disconnected pause, as if they couldn't remember where they were. One of the guitarists, my cousin's cousin Tom, kept a plodding rhythm accompanied by his nodding head; the drummer, lean and silent, just moved things along. The lead guitarist glared at people, then looked to the guitar like he was reading the thing. The guitarist drove the fiddler and the fiddler drove the guitarist in understanding. Smartness is everywhere: at the most routine crap jobs, in backwoods, illiterate places. Sometimes you're born with it, sometimes it comes out of love, sometimes you just work your ass off and get old and know.

growing up with rednecks and punks

And I wasn't one to look up to age. I was impatient with it, and wanted to move as far from hick knowledge as I could get. I thought of my grandpa as outmoded, a little silly even, but he really wasn't old when we held the dances—not the way he got later, when he could no longer sign his name and would wander off at Kmart and be found over by the blue light special wondering if he was in Kansas. When the caller announced the dance, I knew I'd be dragged out there again. Guess he thought it was good for me, but more likely he just needed a partner, since Grandma would never get out in front of people. What would my friends think?—thank God they weren't there! We faced each other. Our paired nature broke to dance with people on either side, and returned when we swung one another again, elbow crook to elbow crook. We passed beneath a canopy of raised arms, a maneuver mimicked in other line dances. Using the lickety-split language of the auctioneer, the caller announced the steps in time to the music. This wasn't particularly instructive to an inept bozo like me. The dance whipped along and without my experienced partner to lead me through the maze I would have been shit out of luck. Grandpa positioned me to swing the one on the right, the one on the left, to get through the line. If I was lucky, I got a gentle hand on the back instead of a yank on my arm.

When you're small and the partner is large, you're swept along, feet barely touching the floor, dizzy from turns and touches. There was no time for thought, let alone self-consciousness. A square dance, as in any partner dance, requires intimacy. Unlike twosome dances, you are held by friends and strangers. Like living in a small town, everyone is webbed and you must exhibit love and trust to get anywhere. The bargain is to accept the whispers and criticism as a sad conjunction to belonging. So in the dance we give up and move through skin, sweat, strength, power, laughter, confusion, and the absolute joy of physical abandonment with common people who live down the road.

DANCING LINES AND SQUARES

I whirled until I was dizzy and breathless, frightened at being pushed, never knowing where I would end, pleased to feel part of the group—not watching, but a link in the line, a corner of the square. Flung hand-to-hand in an elegant loop, I felt like I was being shoved through one of those hard Christmas candies with the squiggles and holes between the squiggles. The very shape of it was old and if there is genetic memory I had it in the sliding and hopping, the bounce on the balls of the feet. I wasn't afraid to hold strangers' hands, and only a little alarmed when I was lifted off my feet and twirled. People who might otherwise leave me shy with their talk of baking or building became partners. Some of the women wore dancing skirts that rose high in the spin, and Keds, flat and slick on the bottom. The men changed when they wore their hats and plaid snap shirts and string ties. They became polite and courtly. If they got drunk, they did it quietly. They bowed to the partner, bowed to the corner. I danced until I was dizzy, a dust devil circling the prairie.

Hearing the fiddle in dance, rather than from a respectful distance, turned it into a possessed force. The inspired fiddler screeched, cried, prayed. In the fevered movement of bow against string was a fight against every rule-driven, ordinary thing. While following the backbone of the traditional song, the fiddler let the music take him where it wanted him to go. This crazy call of string and word pushed me through arms and legs in a sensuous frenzy that maintained the decorum of square and row.

When the dance was over, we sat, catching our breaths. Neighbor yelled to neighbor, bar-style, the news of the day, the weather, the state of their sore feet, or Mabel's bad son. The music slowed, and the songs, rather than creating momentum, reflected upon everything gone.

Called up was the mournful isolation of the Appalachian mountains; old nuggets with names I don't remember along with standards, "Rocky Top," "Orange Blossom Special," "Uncle Pen": homesick songs. Back then, before the market-co-opted "new country," the area preservers-of-tradition played what they'd been raised with. Looking back, as these songs often do, was an act of regret and celebration. The sweet melody of "Uncle Pen" by the greatest recorded fiddler, Bill Monroe, describes the storyteller's bond with his uncle, a fiddler who passed on his gift to the child Bill. "Uncle Pen played the fiddle, lordy how it would ring, you could hear it talk, you could hear it sing." Pen listens for the "call"—the square dance instructions and the calling of musical commitment and God. Many Bill Monroe songs play off the triangle of loving involvement: art, religion, and the people around him. The songs have a delicate melancholy, a tribute to actions past and relationships tentative. The storyteller is aware of passing away.

And that was how it went. Over that summer, I learned to dance a little better, but not much; I've always been an instinct dancer, and didn't like the rules. But my success at the dance didn't matter. What counted was this gathering of people who I would never be much like. I would never fit—never own a pair of cowboy boots or ride a horse or tease my hair. But I understood that fiddler, and knew the mourning ache of the immigrant song. At the dances I felt alone, but close to my cousins; I felt alone, but loved to watch my mother dance with my aunt. Sometimes you don't have to be inside to belong.

When the season turned, the dances ended. I think it was money, money for the hall; but finally nobody cared enough to donate. Or couldn't or didn't find anyone to do the legwork. My uncle was squabbling with his brother, and they never could agree. The old hill animosities were still around, undermining any attempt to pull shit together and build a community that could last. No one in the town volunteered.

WE'RE SO PRETTY

You might've called us punkers, might still. If punk was attitude, we had that; but if it was about annihilation, we never went far enough to embrace it. We were fringe-dwellers. Hanging out, dancing, watching movies that never hit the major theaters. Pipe-smoke ideas circled our heads like spouted verse, and sometimes it really was poetry that took shape as tangible as a lotus and as human as the person across from us. We made mistakes, convinced that the most egregious sins were turns of daring creativity. Our naïveté was unmarred by responsibility. We were young, and stayed young way too long. We danced up and down like corks in the river, fast, faster, until finally washed up to shore.

It was the '70s, after all. What else could I do? I went to discos; I watched the dancers whirl and point. Curled hair, polyester, the whole thing. I was nineteen, barely drinking age, and my friends Cathy and Cindy wanted to pick up guys. Not to sleep with them—we were "good kids" who had gone to a small-town school and knew how to behave—but to be attended to by them. Cindy and Cathy wanted to know that they had briefly dated men who owned restaurants or a dry cleaning store or a plane. It was like they were at a fancy buffet, sampling the offerings in the shiny serving trays. But I couldn't do it. I'm too sincere or something. Too not-slick, too nerdy. Cathy and Cindy thought I needed to get out of the books and into the world. They and I were sure I had a problem.

And then came punk, savoir of intellectual geeks and outcasts. Punk doesn't have the reputation of being for smart people, but that's all wrong. You have to be smart to be that far outside, that isolated, and not be into heavy metal or self-destructive goth. Punk is for nervous people who like lyrics. Punk is for people who couldn't fit and came to like it.

So what's punk? It's new wave, grunge, dada, and the Sex Pistols. It's not just the pin-in-the-nose thing—we never did

175

that. It would have hurt. It's community dancing by jumping up and down, which was later adapted into mosh-pit floating. It has its violent side, but we didn't partake in that, just as we didn't sample every drug that passed our way. We liked the silly, ironic, word-play side. The side of the Talking Heads, Blondie, and, of course, the Ramones.

Joey Ramone is dead. Joey Ramone got cancer at the same time as my mother. Joey Ramone will always be twenty-five, but the obituaries claimed he was forty-seven.

Joey Ramone was the ugliest Ramone, and that's saying a lot. He was also sexy and sublime in his ugliness, an icon for tortured ironic girls. His sweetness transcended the long black hair, crooked glasses, and ripped jeans. Joey had no pose. The Ramones were just a crew of high school drop-outs from New York City. They didn't wear costumes or make-up, didn't play to the press, didn't bullshit—never did, even after their brand of punk faded from the public eye in favor of the slicked-up, more easily marketed versions that get radio play. The Ramones were reassuring. They were guys you could hang out with and depend on. They held the community of Punk in place until we all got older.

Who believes in community now?

We naïve Midwestern punkers fell into three aesthetic groups: those who wore Patti Smith, Iggy Pop, Sex Pistols angst on their t-shirts; those who liked the intellectual literary approach of the Talking Heads and Elvis Costello (while drinking our Tanguerey and tonics); and those who liked the goofy poppy stuff like the Ramones and Blondie because we couldn't take anything seriously. Of course, we still knew plenty of people who listened only to the Eagles and Dan Fogleberg and Joni Mitchell, but we mostly felt sorry for them. They were so timid.

All of these punk preferences mutated into the local bands,

and I knew every one that played in Springfield, Illinois. Our favorite was The Undercovers: four not-that-bright guys led by the skinny, hyper Jim Q. He had already hit thirty and was known to tie his lovers to his bedposts using unwashed white gym socks. He'd get on stage and gyrate and grate to everything from Iggy to the Clash. Looking back, it was pretty sedate—Jim didn't rip off his shirt or smash his guitar—but we thought it was cutting-edge as we leapt about on the floor and got drunk. *We're so pretty, oh so pretty . . . va-cant!* Jim would moan and we figured we were not vacant at all because we got it, we understood that pain of feeling all alone and isolated and messed-up. I ran to these shows with a series of girlfriends and sometimes we'd dance with guys and sometimes with a group of people. Unlike the disco scene, it wasn't a pick-up trip. I went most often with Jae, and we would sit together at some table in the corner and make fun of everyone, as people who secretly want to fall in love with someone are wont to do. Jae had bushy reddish hair and was obsessed about her weight and bad things—bad things from her year at college, bad things from home, bad things even she wasn't in tune with, deep shit bad. I was a good listener. I only had a lot to say if I was drunk. Then I was boring.

Sounds, lights, talk, scratches on the bathroom wall, jokes, slick floor, angel hair: I loved bars, those bars. No form, no mirror balls, no mirrors, nothing to remind me that I was a geek—it was a world of geeks, geeks turned beautiful, geeks in love with the moment.

We drank beer, wine, whiskey, gin, White Russians, schnapps. Sometimes all in one night. I'd help Jae or some other friend home and then would drive to my parents' house where I still lived. And I would run to the bathroom and throw up. Every night. No ambition, time out of time, and people, and place. It was where I found myself then, wound up inside a tornado. I was innocent. I swear.

I met an almost-famous punker, Adrian Belew. He was a high-class session guitarist, a regular with Bowie. We loved him. He was so distant.

He was from Champaign, Illinois, and ended up living back on his home turf. For a few years, he settled in Springfield and formed a new band and played our clubs. We thought we were close to God, being in the same room with and having a conversation with someone who personally knew *David Bowie*. My friend Larry (who later called himself Lars) was in love with him. I wasn't. I wasn't in love with anyone. I hadn't met a soul yet who could sense my thoughts before I spoke. No one I could feel before I could see. No one I moved for, wrote for, danced for. Women and men were in love with Adrian. All of the musicians consumed lovers like candy.

Adrian seemed oblivious. He was a sweet, out-there, and very married kind of guy. Lanky, dark-haired, always smiling, with a farm-boy face. Nothing strange about him; he was simply self-absorbed, the way serious artists tend to be. He was famous for his innovative guitar technique. He played guitar for hours a day, he said.

I crashed a few parties. One was held in his recording studio, a spare cement building on the edge of the city. It was the first punk-party I'd been to where the cocaine was on the table. People who I'd never seen in town before were dressed and hyped up to the hilt. The music, some live and some recorded, bounced off the walls. Everyone was showing off. Contracts were negotiated. Deals wheeled, or trying to be wheeled. We all want to be famous, I realized. We are in the middle of the cornfields and we are so horribly desperate that we will glom onto anyone with the slightest semblance of fame. It was disco all over again. The lights looked like mirror balls. I stood in the corner while everyone scrambled for Adrian's attention. I stood in the corner while we prayed for a word, or at least an autograph. The closer people got, the more perfect they became. We had been so much safer when we didn't know success.

Now Tony—he was punk, though he never accepted this or any label. Like almost everybody who played punk/new wave or hung around the bars, he was strictly your average middle class suburban kind of guy. Known as the Guitar God, he played in Midwestern bands and finally settled in St. Louis, got a job at a library. We met in community college, neither of us knowing what to do, working for Audio-Visual in the basement. Our evenings were spent watching movies in empty classrooms where I saw Fellini's *Satyricon, The Seventh Seal,* even *Bringing Up Baby.* While we spliced film, he and I swapped theories. Certain he was right, Tony talked non-stop about jazz, though what he played was a melancholy sort of power pop. Talking art was what all my friends did, stuck there in the middle of Illinois, drifting along, full of illusions, sure we would all become Big Deals. Beneath the fluorescent lights, while our boss, Brenda, counted the roses she'd gotten from her girlfriend, Tony told me which bands were legit and which were sell-outs. Anyone who sought popularity without ability was a phony. No three-chord wonders for Tony.

I thought he was full of it, this chubby, boyish guy, balding at the age of twenty-three, an in-your-face Italian who let you know in no uncertain terms that Blondie did not have talent, that the real stuff was Stax-Volt, electric blues, complexity, and the rest a corporate scam. . . . Then I heard him play.

We don't like to think of our guitar gods as average shlubs from Chatham, Illinois. We're trained into wasted addicts, big-hair bare-chested hunks, intense English blonds. When Tony played the guitar, dancers stopped to listen. He formed bands, but discarded them because no one was as serious as he needed them to be. While some guys have an overabundance of testosterone, Tony had an overload of integrity. He could not allow himself to be bad. He couldn't wear makeup, wigs, jewelry, safety pins, or anything wilder than a plaid flannel shirt. What's more, he couldn't abide sales tendencies in his band mates.

Too bad he was a real musician. As Greil Marcus said of punkers, rock and roll to them was "a rotting corpse: a monster of moneyed reaction, a mechanism for false consciousness, a system of self-exploitation, a theater of glamorized oppression, a bore." Artistic purity doomed many a punker as she tore down her art form to help it survive. Since rock is a collaboration, a musician has to have charisma and vision to gain the power to run the show, to be the innovator that attracts players to back her. Tony wouldn't give up enough to get what he really needed: stage presence. He wanted music to be high-level, even perfect— and in needing that he lost the fun.

One night after I got back from living in New York, Tony and I and some friends hung out in my parents' basement and we played records. (Yes, *records;* and they sounded better, too. This is before the time of "digitally remastered" when computer reigns supreme, overtaking that sweet treble.) Dusty Springfield, the Beach Boys, Jonathan Richman, the Talking Heads, Curtis Mayfield, James Brown, Arthur Brown, Ruth Brown. . . . We debated the upsides and the downsides. We had the innocent belief that our rebellion, like the anarchical angels', would change mentalities and provide us with our place in the heavens. . . . Post-'60s, '70s kids, we hadn't yet absorbed Ronald Reagan. We believed the pendulum would swing back and didn't know that the only Democratic president in years would get publicly humiliated for being blown in a tiny room, leaving us all, all of us, dirty. . . . When the Sex Pistols sang *I wanna be . . . anarchy* we believed we had been set free from all that, a lawlessness unto ourselves.

But Tony doesn't like that kind of music anymore. The last time we talked, he'd stopped playing—not just his own music, but any other popster's. Tony's songs had been soap bubbles with a consciousness; an echo of the d.b.s., Elvis Costello, Brian Wilson—delicate power punk accompanied by chiming, anxious, and angry guitar. Like me, Tony's in his forties now. "It's for the kids," he told me on the phone. "It's all about performance, and I'm tired. You play and people are talking over you, drinking beer; they don't want to hear, to pay attention. If they'd just let me play without going out there, like if I could just put out a tape. . . ."

Tony came close to touring with a major female star, but it never came off. Maybe it was his lack of ambition, his crabby removal, I'm not sure. Maybe just bad luck. I asked him what kind of music was coming out, back when my daughter was young and I was newly divorced and had little money. I wanted to absorb his musician's life second-hand, hear what was cutting-edge, like when we used to swap tapes for Christmas. "Hate grunge," he said. "Hate rap. Boring. Had to hear that same crap over and over at the shop." (He worked at Vintage Vinyl.) I sat there, phone in hand, watching my daughter walk her Barbie over the arm of the couch, us living in this pit of a basement wondering what was going to happen next, me not even able to afford a CD player, let alone the CDs. The last time I'd seen Tony play, his parents—this really nice Italian pair who were supportive and proud—and his friends and I were cramped together in a bar. We danced all night long, a little drunk, but mostly dizzy on sound and the sheer adrenaline of raucous guitar, leaps and jokes, and being there, among friends, knowing that we knew something, that we had found something. And then it was gone.

I never thought it could be gone for good. A wink in time when we were happy just to be happy. I never believed that rock and roll was really tied in with youth.

And Tony said to me, "Uh, man, I listen to classical now. Jazz, too, but mostly classical. I want to see how they did it. And then I compose in my room. I've learned all I can with rock." Unable to stay with any kind of profession because he still carried that dream, he told me he worked the circulation desk. Never married, no children, forty years old.

It was very hard for us punks to adjust.

One of the bands Tony hated was one of my favorites. X was a group from L.A. with lead singer Exene Cervenka, her husband, John Doe, and assorted band mates. They were too thrasher for Tony, but I liked edge. Violence in music is a representation of who we are. Nobody said music has to show just the upbeat or moody side of existence; it had to show the rage, too. So X, who power-chorded their sunny, disturbed, and destructive California lives, appealed to me; and I liked the fact that they had a powerful chick singer who looked like a Santa Monica beatnik. *I'll just throw my lipstick and bracelets like gravel. . . .* This futile, doom-packed stuff validated what I believed was true: that we (I) could never escape our pasts, we were screwed, screwed up, destined to have accident after accident.

Okay, it was fun to pogo to. . . . Slamming never got to where we lived, downstate among the fields. I didn't get what it was all about until I spent four months in L.A., living in a bungalow with Tim (my ex) and his friend John, a biologist at UCLA. Every day we walked down to an ocean I'd never seen until that summer, and I never could adopt the tan, blond slickness of the people on the beach who knew how to walk on sand without burning their feet. *Like adult books I don't understand, Jackie Susann meant it that way. . . .* That season a storm blew in and the shop windows and signs in Hermosa Beach shattered, leaving gaping holes where a person could just reach in and steal one of a thousand surfboards, boogie boards, Hawaiian-print towels. . . . A sad, sunshiny culture of constant drugs that John's brother would slip in to the bungalow and deal out like cards, while we grilled fat burgers and ate avocados off the tree in the backyard. I was the one who talked them into going to see X at the Roxy.

growing up with rednecks and punks

Weirdly disconnected, the band stared up at the ceiling while the dance turned into a shoving match that pushed me up against a barricade between floor and table area; and a crazy, creepy guy with tattoos and lank dishwater hair followed us around going "Are you Opie? Opie? Richie, where are you, Richie? Let's go home now." My ex and I hid out in the seats and watched the ones who thought they were the real punks, the ones who would hurt you, beat you, steal everything, and enjoy it. The welly-welly-well *Clockwork Orange* punks who would later shave their heads and stop destroying themselves and start destroying everyone else.

A lot of us in Springfield worshiped the poet Vachel Lindsay. Author of "The Congo," bashed now by literary critics, Vachel was the first rock-and-roll punk. A performance artist post–turn of the 20th century, Vachel sang and chanted his poems to awestruck young women, an actual mass audience (poetry had some in those days). He was like Brian Jones, or Jim Morrison, or even Donovan—a poet-slash-mystic-visionary, a bit mad. He believed that Springfield was magical, that Lincoln walked its streets, that ghosts filled his yard. He read myths, made myths of everything and everyone he knew, and illustrated these mythological poems with paintings and line sketches. Vachel tramped the United States giving his poems away, trading rhymes for bread, as he said. A doctor's son, an artist's son, Vachel stayed a child until shortly before he died in middle age. Celibate for years, doting upon his muses, enjoying nothing more than lacing young women's boots, Vachel made the fatal error of marrying and having children. Facing declining success and the brutal ugliness of an unhappy marriage, Vachel's dreamy punkness no longer sustained him. Unable to adjust, move on, mellow, channel, adapt, Vachel drank a bottle of Rid-O-Rats, crawled up the stairs of his childhood home, and died.

Where do they go, all those exuberant dreams? Get shuffled into the work schedule, the joker in the pack waiting to jump out and kick us when we least expect it? Do they go into the garage with the other albums, too out of date to be borne? Get updated with the latest in CDs, SUVs, TVs? Get transferred to the Dreams For Our Children, our own illusions placed in the box and taped?

Forget about fame. Forget about success. Forget about advertising. Forget about Adrian Belew. Forget about fame. . . . Remember Joey Ramone. Joey Ramone is dead at forty-seven. Not of drugs or hard living. Of cancer. Joey, the sweetest of the Ramones, is dead at forty-seven.

When the Ramones had their farewell tour a few years before, the critics all laughed. Farewell, sure . . . we'll see. Hardly anyone knew that Joey was dying. The contract was written and signed.

Punks believed that life should be intense and interesting and funny, because . . . we were all gonna die. Oh sure, we *said* it, but who believed it? We thought we were so clever, with that punk irony and angry nihilism. But there's a time when the pointlessness of anger hits us in the face. What's to say about anger, finally, but that it's there? Glasses get thrown, the guitar smashed, and then, well, that's it. Giving in, seeing it, we're left with a couple of options. We can die an actual death or a living one, or we can move on. We can live in our parents' basements, playing music on the weekends, waiting for the break we know won't come, or we can transfer our dreams to our children, or we can channel. Maybe we'll get a really good job, a profession that sustains us, defines us, and transfers our old punkness into productivity. Or we'll put it into something complicated and philosophical, maybe even politically motivated. When we finally figure out that Joey is our brother, then we'd better be like Tony, the Guitar God, and transform and transmute into the complexities of jazz, better start improvising and fast, better stop worrying about profit, and notice the moment.

In my room is a laptop keyboard, the sounds of my daughter walking upstairs, books by friends and strangers, a beaten lamp, a coffee cup, a poster of Woodstock, and a boom box (silent for the moment) that plays bluegrass and country and funk and punk, all on CDs. The room is in the basement, which smells faintly of mildew, and bells hang from a dresser mirror because my daughter put them there. This is now. Don't look back. Joey Ramone is dead.

Turn the page fast.

getting
out to
other places

STARS ON
HOLY WATER

I SAT WITH MY FEET UP on the dash while Doug pulled the van into the parking lot of the Doubletree Inn in Lowell, Massachusetts. I'd nearly forgotten the visions of Lowell delivered to me fifteen years ago in those Kerouac novels: his lyrical descriptions of a water-built, working-people's city. Catholicism, spiritualism, early death, and fantasies of being on the road haunted those books. In that younger, more untested time in my life, I'd loved Kerouac's writing, full of place and the well-meaning people I'd grown up with. Back when I idolized Kerouac as much as he idolized Cassidy and Ginsberg and the other real people he turned into myths, I imagined visiting Lowell. I admired the way the city was holy to him. This I understood, coming from a rural river home, where water led to dreams and daydreams and a sense of endless motion.

My childhood settled among the trees and brushes of the Sangamon River; Kerouac's, along the Merrimack. Kerouac's Lowell was a haphazard immigrant city, full of sinners, workers, loneliness, and claim. The transport I found in nature came for him in the people he met and in the religious mysticism that made all seem significant. Not being Catholic, I didn't grasp his search for heaven in humans, or his sense of the icon; though I did understand God in everything small, in the way my grandmother, who wanted to be a nun, tended her flower beds with meticulous love. Jack Kerouac sped around the country, his vision encompassing the big picture, a pining for discovery turning the real into story. I, too, had this restlessness, and at forty I found myself in Kerouac's home town. That his death was brought on by liquor and disappointment didn't stop me from wanting to live big and know how he had lived.

If Lowell had its good side of the tracks, I couldn't find it. The city's primary industry, the textile mills, was mostly closed down. Beyond Jack Kerouac, Lowell was noted for its mill girls— the first women industrial laborers in the U.S., hired in the 1800s to run the looms. Their legacy was the empty, broken-windowed factories that backdropped downtown.

All signs led to Boott Mill, and it was in this direction that Doug, the kids, and I headed the next day. Lowell's streets were clotted with restless drivers as we dodged through a quiet, oddly waiting downtown. Locals leaned against storefronts and sat in restaurant chairs as they watched traffic pass them by. My impression of the looming mills was less industrial oppression than quaintness. The factory buildings were three-story brick enclaves with steeples, reminiscent of Harvard. Only smokestacks undermined the industrialists' attempts at Eastern decorum. This comparison to the university is not so incongruous; many of the Lowell "mill girls" sought learning along with wages. Country women hunting adventure and knowledge, immigrants coming for the American dream, and Kerouac's search for spirit were intertwined as neatly as Lowell's merging one-way streets.

The park rangers at the Visitors Center were congenial men and women in brown uniforms and Yogi Bear hats. A friend of mine had been a ranger on the Lincoln beat, and I knew that the park employee's life was a clean, polite, federal one; being historians, they understood the cities where they worked.

One of the rangers told me about Kerouac's grave and favorite bars, and gave me a rundown on mill history. The Lowell factories opened in the 1820s, when women were hired from the surrounding countryside to run the looms. The workers, as young as ten and as old as sixty, stood on their feet eleven hours a day. (In later years, the shifts went thirteen hours; after unsuccessful strikes, the Yankee women quit, replaced by cheaper and more compliant immigrant labor.) Strapped by circumstance— the death of parents, the need to support siblings, conflicts at home, or simple restlessness—the girls (as they called themselves) from the White Mountains eagerly met the call for workers. In Lowell they lived in boardinghouses run by the mills. Their home lives were regimented in strict dormitory style to protect them from "vice" and to fight off critics of the factory system: work all day, lights out at ten, compulsory church attendance on their only day off.

As we walked through the Visitors Center, my sixteen-year-old stepdaughter, Monica, looked over the displays. Her interest came from a book she'd read about a mill worker, Lyddie. Monica, with her protected life, had compassion for people who were badly treated; her sense of factory existence was that it was sheer brutality, and she pitied the girls. Since she had enough advantages and smarts to never be poor, she looked at the mills through the lenses of righteous feminism and distant comprehension of repetitive physical work. My curiosity about the mills was different: my dad worked in factories all his life, and I'm always trying to put my lunchbox, graveyard shift–laden childhood together with my professional life. I had a lot of tedious jobs—at a paper bag factory, a Dairy Queen, and as a clerk in libraries and offices, among other things—and know about the tenuousness of money and the drone of monotony. I identify with the workers in a way that Monica will never have to. Because of this I found myself more attracted to the streets than the tours; and maybe so I wouldn't have to think too much about my laboring past I spent a lot of time talking to Jack Kerouac.

Before I met Jack, the ranger told me about the working people's museum, the Boott Mills tours, and Kerouac Park on Bridge Street. "I didn't like the guy's books myself," he said. "Didn't make a whole lot of sense." I asked him who mostly came to see the Kerouac sites. "Now that's a funny thing." He seemed about ready to wink, like he really enjoyed talking to a woman. "It's mostly the Italians. Don't know why, but Italians love him. And the Canadians. They make a pilgrimage. Other than that, not too much."

It had been so long since I'd read Kerouac that I'd forgotten he was bilingual. In his family, Kerouac was "'Ti Jean"; he grew up in the Lowell neighborhood then known as Little Canada. It wasn't possible to visit Kerouac's childhood haunts because Little Canada had been destroyed for the intercity highway. The French were pretty far down the Lowell pecking chain, as each new immigrant population took the bottom rung and the oldest climbed up. The Greeks thought well of themselves in Kerouac's day, although in the factory girls' time, Yankees had the leg up. By the late 1800s, English women were displaced by Irish men. Asians (Cambodians, Laotians, and Vietnamese) arrived after the Vietnam war, not long after, the Puerto Ricans and the Portuguese. The sidewalks were full of young people with honey-colored skins.

After I thanked the chatty park ranger and went leafing through the books at the Visitors Center, Kerouac made his appearance. I wasn't expecting him—the guy was dead, after all—and I thought I'd moved way past him. The loose lyricism of his books gave me a compulsive desire to edit, clean him up and make him tidy. I've even gotten irritated at Kerouac, because my students haul in *On the Road* and tell me it's okay to write whatever comes into their heads and that it's sacrilegious to revise a word of their (hit-and-miss) golden prose. I tell them that the only book of Kerouac's that got much attention was *On the Road*. He was put aside when he couldn't embrace the streams of '60s change and the demands of writing a conventionally edited book; he became a cliché, a symbol of a Beat movement that he never desired or believed in. Students roll their eyes. Of course, they're right. It would be great if art were really free.

I skipped past *On the Road* and picked up a Lowell story about growing up immigrant and outside, about the moment of love that's full of belief, before it's beset by cynicism and dismay.

This Kerouac was not about travel and amphetamines, but

getting out to other places

understood what it was like to grow up near water, in a place where roughness was the landscape. From *Maggie Cassidy:*

> And at night the river flows, it bears pale stars on the holy water, some sink like veils, some show like fish, the great moon that once was rose now high like a lazing milk flails its white reflection vertical and deep in the dark surgey mass wall river's grinding bed push. As in a sad dream, under the streetlamp, by pocky unpaved holes in dirt, the father James Cassidy comes home with lunchpail and lantern, limping, red-faced, and turns in for supper and sleep.
>
> Now a door slams. The kids have rushed out for the last play, the mothers are planning and slamming in kitchens, you can hear it out in swish leaf orchards, on popcorn swings, in the million-foliaged sweet wafted night and sighs, song, shushes. A thousand things up and down the street, deep, lovely, dangerous, aureating, breathing, throbbing like stars; a whistle, a faint yell; the flow of Lowell over rooftops beyond; the bark on the river, the wild goose of the night yakking, ducking in the sand and sparkle; the ululating lap and pull and lovely mystery on the shore, dark, always dark the river's cunning unseen lips murmuring kisses, eating night, stealing sand, sneaky.
>
> "Mag-gie!" the kids are calling under the railroad bridge where they've been swimming. The freight train still rumbles over a hundred cars long, the engine threw the flare on little white bathers little Picasso horses of the night as dense and tragic in the gloom comes my soul looking for what was there that disappeared and left, lost, down a path—the gloom of love. Maggie, the girl I loved.

That was when Kerouac tapped me—

Not Kerouac, the shy jock romantic. But the boozy, tired Kerouac of the later Lowell years. He started telling me this long story about Lowell High School, and how Duke had been the best football player he'd ever met. Then he clapped a hand on my shoulder. "What's a woman like you doing reading books like this?" he laughed, or rather guffawed in that big-mouthed, showy way of guys who drink too much. Like a lot of working-class men, his view of women wasn't real progressive. He'd turn on me and lambaste me to his buddies in a second.

"I like the Lowell stuff. I like your description of the town and the people."

"All places are Lowell. Lowell is all about America. Look at what we got: Greeks, Canadians, Irish, Eye-talians, English, Germans, Puerto Ricans, and now we got the boat people, though that was after I'd kicked out of here. Everybody trying to find something. God on the shores of the New World."

"Sure, Jack, *but*." I pulled him aside, toward the posters. He looked like a bum in his rumpled jacket and rain hat; and—the ranger's frown told me—this was a Visitors Center, not a place for sloppy locals. "You can't tell me the immigrants aren't disappointed."

"Hey. They got what they want. They got possibility. That's all people need."

"Bullshit, you are so full of it. People need food, a place to stay—"

"They got shelter. They're not starving. The place they left, they didn't have enough to eat. Maybe the authorities were after them. This freedom thing is real. It's where a factory worker can be a poet, sister."

His eyebrows scrunched—sizing me up, like I wasn't appreciating my own life.

"Jack. This town's, well, I hate to put it to you this way, but it's a notch above a slum."

"*Slum!*"

My formerly friendly park rangers went stone-faced. The tourists—a white-haired couple from California and school kids waiting for the slide show to start—turned. The kids laughed and pointed, eager for a fight. The old folks headed for the doors. "You think it has something to do with money!" Kerouac bellowed. "Freedom is beyond the crass exchange of bill and coin. It's a toehold, man, the spot to jump from, all a person needs—"

"Easy to say if you don't have kids." I glanced at my daughter who was flipping through books of Dover paper dolls. She watched me out of the corner of her eye, as if she never knew what kind of trouble I was going to get myself in. "Nobody wants to raise their kids in a one-room apartment. Or with people looking down on them."

Kerouac fidgeted with the buttons of his coat. "I concede your point about the unfairness thing. Look, I don't have a college education. I went to a Jesuit school, and they taught me everything. College just seemed a lot of empty words between people from another country. I went to Columbia for a year on a football scholarship—"

"I went for a year, too," I butt in. While I was there, my ex kept threatening to jump out the window of our apartment building.

"I was a physical being in a mental world, but I finally saw through all that. But"—he looked me in the eye "—I could've done it. If I'd wanted."

"Let's go for a walk."

I told Doug I was scouting on my own, without the kids, if that was okay, to get a sense of the place. He said fine, not paying much attention to Kerouac; he's a pretty secure guy, and even literary idols don't faze him. Kerouac politely held open the door, eyeing my ass while he did it. A '50s fella, he hadn't re-formed into subtlety.

"The mills." Kerouac gestured at the brick face dominating the skyline. "They're what Lowell's about. The chance to make a buck. Hard-work babies rising up the food chain."

"I want to see the factories." To feel where the mill girls had worked the loud, grinding machines in humid rooms full of plants.

"Why? I wouldn't. I won't." He stared toward the horizon of rectangles, then took my arm. "Let's drink."

I sighed. Somewhere inside this bloated, red-nosed Kerouac was the wild-hearted guy I'd always imagined. But I came too late. This was the Kerouac who no longer wrote; his last book, *Vanity of Dulouz,* barely sold. He hid with cats in his mother's house, drinking and avoiding Ginsberg and Corso and the rest. He died of cirrhosis of the liver when he was only forty-eight. I'd imagined the declining Kerouac as silent and taciturn, but he was boisterous, talking so loud that everyone who passed us on the street heard what he had to say. When I met his eyes again— Kerouac! my literary hero!—I wished he were still the intense man who watched the world pass by at parties, sitting in the corner with a jug in his hand. I wished I were not so old, and I wished I didn't care.

In a sprinkling of rain, we walked downtown. Lowell was a city of canals, and we crossed the first of many bridges spanning the Merrimack. The river flowed the way a river does, prepared to work, slowed and squeezed by locks. The canals weathered by adaptation. It wasn't a pastoral river, but was intent on getting where it needed to go; no one paused to watch it pass, or to eat lunch at the water's edge. Like the river, they had things to do. The pace was slow, for an Eastern city; people stood on the sidewalks at midday, or called to one another from corners, or kissed, pressed against buildings. Off the bridge and on the sidewalk and into the thick of things, I heard accents and saw colors that never appeared in such condensed variety in the Midwest. A young woman leaned against a coffee shop wall, smoking a cigarette; she eyed my Liz Claiborne shirt (not knowing I had bought it secondhand) and my Levis and my Timberland sandals; she had on a pink waitress uniform and her face was as soft and pale as biscuit dough. On the next corner was a Hispanic kid on a bike; down the street, a thin Asian man in a nicely pressed white shirt looked out the window of a restaurant. A lady with teased red hair smiled from behind the counter of the dollar store, remembering me from an hour before when I'd stopped to buy scrunchies for my daughter's ponytail. All the while, Kerouac was saying, "It didn't used to be like this, this used to be part of Greek town and woe to all who were not Greek. Every year some new type comes in and I can't keep them straight. The Puerto Ricans, the Portuguese, and now the Laotians and what have you, for Chrissake—hey, look out, there's—" He pulled my arm lest I step in something on the sidewalk, spilled or puked-up gunk. His grip was firm for someone who looked like he'd been on a lifelong bender, and I realized that because a man was dying didn't mean he was weak.

"That makes it kind of interesting," I said.

He threw a friendly arm around my shoulder. "Sure, what's to change? We like it this way. It's ours, that's why we're here. Who needs that generic white-bread name-brand insurance-executive world when you have paradise?" And he moved his arm wide to encompass it. The Greek restaurants (run by Greeks), Oriental food suppliers, hardware stores (run by Italians), dress shops with cheap polyester lime-green shirts and plastic platform shoes (about which my husband had said, "Is everything here a Goodwill?")—and good, cheap places to get food. A small Barnes & Noble served as the U-Mass bookstore—the only bookstore, other than the federal park displays. Each place announced its ethnic identity, holding on to what it could of the old culture.

The mill girls wrote of the end of their country ways and their blossoming—or hardening—into city women. They told of the loss of twangs; no one wanted to seem a rube. They mourned the loss of contemplative streams and mountains, while admitting there was time enough to think while running a loom. They let go of the home ways. Maybe these immigrants would, too.

I tried to tell Kerouac about the girls, but he was busy peering through the glass of every storefront and restaurant, like he was looking for somebody. He opened a dirty screen door, flimsy on its hinges. "Time for greasy pizza."

At Sal's, cooks shifted behind metal counters. People—some rumpled, like they'd just gotten out of bed, some gesturing and full of spunky argument, others prim and patient—waited at round tables. The woman behind the counter taking orders and running the cash register yelled at the pizza maker to hurry his ass up. "And this goddamn pizza here, it's so lopsided it won't fit on the plate." She scooted the thing around, but dough still hung over the edges, and she shoved it at the customer, a smiling Hispanic man. The clerk had long fingernails a shade more purple than her thick hair.

The pizza man yelled out to the room, "You guys got complaints?"

"No!" came back a chorus, with bemused snickers, and they dove back into their food.

"See there," the pizza man said to the woman. "So shut your damn mouth and mind your business."

Kerouac and I placed our orders and sat in the corner near the window. I ordered Snapple, because no place in that town had iced tea, let alone iced coffee. There were no bagels or vegetarian delis or even a Dunkin' Donuts. Maybe these were on some secret outskirt of the city, in the vicinity of that ever-present mall or Wal-Mart, but I hadn't seen anything like that driving in.

Kerouac left me to regale some men at another table; a guy's guy, he needed their attention more than a woman's. Who knew what he was telling them. His jacket looked like it had been slept in, possibly on a few lawns.

I put my feet up on the chair, an old habit I've tried to give up since becoming a teacher. My jeans have given way to slacks and skirts, and I wear makeup in recognition of both my age and respectability. Like the mill girls, I adapted. America, for all its

getting out to other places

prideful statements of multi-voicedness, really likes to be all the same. On our trip to New England, my family made stops at Salem, Portsmouth, and Boston. The peaked houses, cramped yards, brick streets—the order and propriety—told of a desire for control, cleanliness, precision. Making a new land was like straightening the bedroom; the bed had to be made, the clutter cleared (of brush, natives), the peculiar not allowed to blossom in the hidden areas. Immigrants got stuffed into their own cities and areas of cities, where communities grew and identity was molded. The Greeks may have beaten on the French, the French on the Portuguese, but none met the standards of Yankee New England. I was on the bottom, growing up. I'm still surprised that you can end up on the bottom by accident of birth, or famine, or war, or bad timing, and that none of this has anything to do with you as an individual. Every time I took the Pledge of Allegiance, I believed. So did my family. The lives they built for themselves were so much better than their hungry childhoods and their parents' childhoods. And thinking about my dad at the factory, and my mom scrubbing the floor reminded me of something.

"Kerouac," I said, when he got the pizza and came back to the table to gobble it up, "how could you stay a patriot through the Vietnam war? You're like my dad, Mr. American Legion." It was the question I'd wanted to ask since I'd read his biography, years ago.

He glared from under his eyebrows and chewed.

"Nobody has the right to burn the flag," he finally said, echoing my family's post-supper political assertions. "You got to be crazy to attack your own home."

"Even when there are principles?"

"Fuck principles!" he bellowed. "Loyalty. Freedom. That's what counts in the pinch. Right, guys?"

"Right!" laughed the men. Kerouac was a real character, they were thinking. He probably bought lots of rounds.

STARS ON HOLY WATER

199

One of them squinted at me. In his mid-twenties, he was plump and pale, with shaggy black hair and the kind of white t-shirt my brother used to wear day in and day out. He said, "Hey, you. We was having this debate. I say it's wrong that in jail they only let us take three showers a week. I say that stirs up a lot of unrest. What do you think?"

His friend, a skinny Italian with a cap, giggled into his pizza. Something embarrassed came in the way he ducked and shook his head, like he thought they should be more polite to women strangers.

"I agree," I said. "That only makes sense."

"See there." He smacked the table, keeping half an eye on me, the tourist.

It had been a long time since I'd hung out with people like this. The ones I'd known before had been in on drug charges, petty thefts. They'd just as soon strip the tires off your car as look at you. Poverty didn't turn most people into Jesus; it made them take what they could because they needed it. But maybe this guy was bullshitting me, and hadn't been in jail at all.

Kerouac wagged a finger. "You wouldn't take more than three baths a week if you were home. Why do you need such luxury in jail?"

"Hey, blow it out your ass, who asked you."

When I was nineteen, I played cribbage in a neighborhood bar with just such a man. I'd heard he'd been in prison, but I never knew for what. He was full of bluster, but was usually gracious. Sometimes people with the hardest lives have the most natural kindness. I couldn't tell about this man, though. Or about Kerouac, for that matter. Alcohol, I knew, obliterated the most lyrical souls.

When we walked to Kerouac Park, my literary compatriot refused to go further. He stared toward the marble slabs where excerpts of his fictions were engraved. His hat, the kind of rain hat old men wear on vacation, was pulled low; I couldn't see his eyes. "My words weren't supposed to be carved."

Without a goodbye Kerouac took his leave and headed off down the canal walkway. He got by alone, used words to keep someone like me from getting too close. I'd really been wanting the young Kerouac anyway, so I could remember when I was young too and rode all night for the adventure; when I could have made these canals Venice. Enough knocks and you see a factory town full of indentured labor and another writer who couldn't get where he wanted to be. Words had to sing and fly in a place like Lowell, where life was kept on a time punch, and getting ahead meant having a place to live and enough change to go to McDonald's. I wished I'd had the courage to chase him down and ask him what it really meant to be on the road and not get hurt, to experience it for its own sake—so enraptured that no one would be able to get to you, to make obscene the wild heart inside. How did you do it? I wanted to call out. Tell me what kept the mill girls' dreams flying. But Kerouac the ghost was already heading home to his ghost cats and a final book of lost visions. He'd probably forgotten anyway, like the rest of us.

LAST TRAIN

Here we come, walkin'
Down the street.
We get the funniest looks from
Ev'ry one we meet.

WHILE SITTING ON A Lewistown, Pennsylvania, train platform, I met Davy Jones of the Monkees. Okay, I didn't actually *meet* him, but he did walk past me, looking as rumpled and seedy as a track bum. In fact, he was the only person on the platform who made me nervous.

After a week of central Pennsylvania, I had grown accustomed to odd characters and strange situations and should have been prepared. Since the place seemed as askew and quirky and set-back-in-time as a '60s sitcom, it figured I'd run into proof that *The Monkees* and *Petticoat Junction* really existed. It was like uncovering a lost tribe of Gilligans who'd settled down with Mary Anns.

Seven days before, on the Fourth of July, I'd been dumped from an Amtrak onto this same train platform. The so-called Lewistown Station was guarded by three guys in cowboy boots. One may have been paid to be there, although it was hard to tell. The building was circled with yellow warning tape because of "renovations," and the bus that had been cheerfully promised when I bought my ticket was nowhere in sight. I knew from growing up in a little town that everything but the tavern would be closed. There'd be no hotel, no mass transportation, maybe not even a place to buy a Coke.

The three guys in lawn chairs grinned at each other. Lugging my bags across the wooden slats of the platform, I walked around the building, still looking optimistically for a door that would open into something ordinary. I walked back.

"When does the bus come by?"

One redneck scratched his black beard and grinned. Another got up, limped a few feet ahead of me, and pointed. "Pay phone's right there."

"But the woman said there was a bus . . . ?"

The grandfatherly one shifted his weight and said, "Ain't been a bus by here in two years that I know of. Ain't that right, Mike?"

"You're right, Jim."

I'd been in enough diners to know that these guys were internally laughing their asses off, and that half the reason they hung around the train platform was to watch city dopes like me wander around asking dumb questions. Much the way these guys would stumble through a big city, which they'd be smart enough never to enter.

"Only bus I know of is Greyhound, about two miles down that way. To the stop sign and make a left and keep going." Mike pointed to an intersection with a factory building on one side and a clapboard house on the other.

I looked at my two heavy bags, considered my four herniated disks, and was struck again by the fact that this was the Fourth of July and I might get to the station and find the doors locked, if indeed there was a bus station that actually had buses. "Is there a phone?"

"Sure. See that pole?"

"Does it have a phone book?"

The guys looked at each other.

"Don't think so."

"The phone to the cab is 358-0001, right?"

"No, I'm pretty sure it's 258."

"Last time I checked it was 358."

"You're wrong, Larry."

I left the guys to discuss it and dug for change. After a few miscues and a dwindling number of quarters, I got the cab company's answering machine. I left a message and stood around wondering what the hell I was going to do if there were no taxis on the Fourth in a town that likely had no hotels, no buses, and no trains going anywhere but New York and Chicago. I put my faith in voice mail and waited.

getting out to new places

Across the tracks rose a tree-covered hill; the town was sheltered by mountains that protected and isolated it. All the buildings looked as weathered and beaten as the decrepit station. The old guys took beer out of the cooler and stared toward the tracks.

That was when I remembered the Hooterville train station. Back in my three-channel childhood, the station in the TV show *Petticoat Junction* was run by a crotchety old bastard and his three lovely nieces, Billie Joe, Bobbie Joe, and Betty Joe. My country name is Becky Jo. (Or Becky Jo-Yo, as my relatives called me, or B.J.) No dignified Rebeccas for me. I could have been a Hooterville sister. Petticoat Junction was one of a group of TV sitcoms about rural life, nearly all of them silly: *Green Acres, The Andy Griffith Show, The Real McCoys.* . . . Sometimes characters from one show would visit the other, small-town folks driving down the road and into our living rooms. Everyone on these shows was nice, and if he wasn't, he was just mildly cranky. Just havin' fun, like these guys at the tracks.

I watched way too much TV as a kid. I believed in TV more than I did real life.

Petticoat Junction and the rest of the country shows had pigs and feed store hats and, well, hooters. They left out the wife-beaters, the drunks (Mayberry, at least, had one of those), the poor, and the prejudiced; well, they left out anyone to be prejudiced toward, since everyone was white. As a kid, I was sure that Hooterville, with its cute eccentrics, must be the real country, and the place where I was living was just screwed up. Hooterville grew Daisy Mae women and Hoss men who walked around chewing hay stalks and falling in love; there wasn't a hint of sex, or even procreation. Even the farmyard animals were chaste. Nobody ever tipped the cows. The skies were blue and the problems funny miscommunications; there were no tornadoes, droughts, lost limbs due to accidents, or foreclosures. It gave me a beautiful lie so that I, gullible child, could hold on while the world around me seethed with trouble. There was, admittedly, something creepy about Uncle Joe, who was supposed to be crabby in a lovable way, except that he kept leering at his nieces. But I ignored my doubts and bought into the illusion of an ideal small-town Hooterville, just as, stepping off the train in Lewistown, I believed that these men in folding chairs were nice harmless guys. A late baby boomer raised on cotton candy, I truly believe that the world is a community of benevolent characters who will make it all turn out right at the end. Love will reveal itself as an innocent surprise, and family is everyone who knows me. I am not alone.

Sweating in the hundred-degree heat, I leaned against the pay phone, thinking what an idiot my husband already thought I was for taking the train when any rational person would have flown and would be there by now. And what was I doing about it? Watching reruns in my head.

I walked back to the train-gazers. "Do you think the cab runs today?" I asked, expecting a really bad answer.

"Oh, yeah, I imagine he'll be out."

"Sure, I'd think so."

"Course, I ain't actually seen him out, have you?"

"Nope. Ain't been downtown today, though."

The guys pegged me as a city girl with too much luggage, which in fact I was, but only recently. So I got out some bubble gum and started chewing, like it would make me look earthy.

"Here comes a freight." The rumble was barely audible.

"Conrail, I imagine."

"Really tying up the lines lately."

About that time, a rattly blue truck pulled into the parking lot.

"Looks like your cab's here."

"Or maybe it's that bus you were talking about."

And there it was: "Scotty's Taxi," letter-stenciled on the side of the door.

getting out to new places

Scotty was the kind of wiry old guy who ate mounds of mashed potatoes and fried chicken and spent his free time in an easy chair and never gained weight because he was full of nervous energy. He loaded my bags into the back of the van. "Should I sit in front?" I asked, since it was just me and Scotty and it would seem rude to sit so far behind him.

"Sure. Up front'll do." I climbed in. Creaky, rusty, with beaten upholstery and cracked vinyl everything, I was reminded of the wreck my dad drove. Source of laughter from my other relatives, Dad's truck required a number of tricks to get it started, had seats that sat up high, and reeked (like Scotty's claptrap) of stale cigarette smoke. Dad's truck also smelled like gas, making me suspect that it was about to blow up. Its glove compartment liked to pop open and the cab was littered with gum wrappers and tools, the ashtray heaped with butts and the plastic wrap from packs of Lucky Strikes. The stick shift switched from gear to gear only with an unusual amount of elbow grease. Yet Dad drove that truck long after it should've been added to a pile of twisted metal.

Scotty's truck was also like Dad's in this regard. "Barely" meant movement, however, and it groaned and shook all the way up the mountain. With common-sense graciousness, Scotty gave me the lowdown on the Lewistown area (and five other podunk towns we passed through on the way to State College). He even introduced the mountain: "See that there," he said, lighting up a cigarette. "We'll be going up that whole thing. Then we'll be going down it. Then we'll go up another one. I bet a girl from Illinois don't see too many mountains."

"I bet she don't," I agreed. I leaned toward the window to get a little of the hot breeze. Scotty had no air conditioning and the digital clock at Lewistown's only bank read 102 degrees (and never gave the time).

"We like it."

"So there's fishing?"

"River passes through. Streams. Go up every weekend. Some people every day."

"Hunting?"

"Everybody hunts. Squirrel, deer, duck."

I thought of my cousin Kirk's arsenal of rifles and pistols, the boat he hauled into the backwaters. Every good day, the men brought back dead woodland creatures. Wild meat tasted tough and sharp, nothing like store-bought chickens. I could never eat a wild animal without thinking of it running free until the moment it was killed. Maybe creatures lost their identity in captivity, brainwashed by routine into hunks of bland, shrink-wrapped meat. Kind of like apartment living.

We drove in silence past houses snuck in among forests, abandoned industrial storehouses, horse barns. "Keep an eye out, we're coming up on the reservoir." We went past a lake like all the lakes in Illinois that provided water for cities. A body of placid fakery.

"Nice," I said.

"Then you get around this area, you got your couple-hun-dred-thousand-dollar houses. But you could get a real house here for fifteen, twenty thousand, a fixer-upper. No jobs, you don't make much around here, but it ain't like there's a cost of living."

"This used to be a coal mining area?"

"Yep, mines."

"All closed down?"

"Yeah."

"So people drive to the city for jobs?"

"No. We got a few stores. Do okay. Ain't no cost of living."

A place for people who want to hide. Or who'd always been there and always would be. Someone who hated Pennsylvania told me that ninety percent of the people who lived there had been born there. This was seen as a mark of failure, since the only way to move up is to move on. Knowing people through generations is nostalgic, backwards, and self-limiting: definitely Hooterville-like. Funny.

I had a friend with big dreams of being a successful writer, who would leave Springfield for a few months, only to come back and take some temporary job. As her writing stayed local, her dreams of fame grew until her vision of becoming a writer turned into a construction of glorious imaginary dinner meetings in New York where she'd meet Prince and Woody. Unable to face the scrapping reality of getting over, she consoled herself with a version of success so out of reach that she could face her choice to stay put. She blamed her kids for keeping her stuck. Like the guys on the train platform, she watched the people go by.

This attitude isn't limited to little town people, though. When I lived in New York City, I met a young woman from Long Island who admitted that her rich father had gotten her into the writing program and that she really wasn't very good at anything. One day, standing outside the doors of Dodge Hall, a building that was surprisingly worn for being part of a hotshot campus, she shyly asked, "What is it like to drive away?"

"What?" I'd never heard of such a question.

"I don't know how to drive. I can't imagine what it must be like to just get in a car and go. I've never been away from here. What do you do with all that . . . space? How do you know where to stop?"

And it struck me that Manhattan was full of people who had lived there their whole lives and would never move away . . . just like. . . .

"So have most of the people always lived around Hootervi— Lewistown? And their grandparents and great-grandparents?"

"Spent my whole life here," he said. "Except two years in Texas. Really liked Texas."

That was probably when he was in the service, which was

usually the only time small-town men left home. That had been true of all of my male relatives, including my brother in the Air Force. Volunteers, they needed the ensured job and duty in order to take the risk. I wanted to ask Scotty about Texas, but felt it might be too personal and maybe even sad and so I looked out the window instead.

By the time we got to the town of State College, Scotty's truck rattled like it was dropping parts. As the name implies, State College existed for teenagers, with strip-malls selling Gap clothes, hemp jewelry, beer, and sandwiches. No good coffee shops, though. "That place has gotta be somewhere. . . ."

We went past hotel after hotel. It was me who spotted the sign for the conference center, a white fake-colonial. Scotty pulled into the circle drive.

"Have a real nice meeting," he said, dumping my bags onto the cement.

"You too, have a nice, uh, time." Knowing he'd be going back to shuttle drunks from the Gold Mine Tavern. But I couldn't say he didn't have the better deal, since I'd be hanging out with academics, working for a place and the esteem that I'd never get. Scotty didn't care for that and didn't need it. While I was sitting beneath fluorescent lights trying to look intellectual, Scotty'd be fishing at a mountain stream, looking at the sky.

On the cab ride back to Lewistown, Phil, a curly-haired, weathered man around forty, gave me the low-down. "Those goddamned baby students who ought to be home with their moms took over the whole town. Everybody hates 'em, imported in from New York and Jersey and every damned place and the school was supposed to be for Pennsylvania kids, man, the kids from around here. These spoiled jerks come down on football scholarships and they don't give a shit, don't have any respect, and the people in State College even put up barriers in the neighborhoods to keep 'em out. The police take the roadblocks down and the people put 'em right back up." It didn't take long to figure out that the "they" Phil was talking about were black and Hispanic. In the '60s, those folks stayed way out of Hooterville. In the '70s, somebody gave them their own shows in the big city and that's the way it oughta be (I heard Phil say underneath what he really did say), so the channel can be changed. "Now we don't mind the Asians—guess you probably noticed there's a big Asian group here—because the Asians work. They mind their own business, don't cause trouble. The Puerto Ricans and the rest, now that's something else." Phil tried to convince me that he wasn't racist—"now it's not *me* who thinks this"—but that it was a practical matter of trouble-types versus the obedient sorts who blend. I knew there'd be no changing Phil's mind; all I could do was talk about my black students and the side of trying to "fit in" that they had to tell. But Phil had heard this talk before and switched to arms.

"Nobody's taking my guns from me. The government tries, but let 'em come to my door, anyone's door around here, and they'll see what happens. We won't have none of that Waco shit around here." Phil wasn't a local; originally from Pittsburgh, he'd spent years hanging around Daytona Beach, then finally settled in central Pennsylvania to escape "the rat race." "It's fine when you're twenty-seven; twenty-seven, you wouldn't've caught me in a place like this. But it hits you that it doesn't add up, you're just working and running around chasing your tail and it's pointless. Here people do what they want and it's their business." Phil told me about his gun collection and about the game (not football, but wild game), and how college was a waste of time. I couldn't imagine Phil married with a family, and he didn't mention one, although I could see him with a live-in girlfriend and a bunch of dogs in a cluttered shack that needed a paint job. I'd known other people like Phil who didn't mind having a crappy job because a job was just there to make the minimal getting-by money that would allow them to do what they really wanted to do, like drink beer. "Everyone here's on welfare," he told me.

Like southern Illinois, where I'd lived for awhile, the coal mines shut down, leaving the workers and their families with nothing. But the people stayed, hanging at the gas stations, bars, bait shops. I'd say it was okay and they were happy and didn't need money, except in southern Illinois I saw beaten-up women, drug-addled guys, abused kids, and heard about murders, suicides, overdoses. Poverty never promotes health and happiness. I was robbed twice in the few months I lived in coal country. Still, few people I met had any desire to leave. They played music, talked big, smoked pot, hung out watching the stars in the unobstructed sky. They lived off government aid, ate government cheese and canned food, played the Grateful Dead, and let their kids run the unfenced countryside. What Hooterville really was was a white ghetto of coal miners who had no place to mine, and farmers whose land had been bought by corporations. Once-idyllic views dug apart by strip mines. "There's Uncle Joe, he's a moving kinda slow at the Junction," said the TV show theme song; of course he was moving slow. There was nothing to do and no place to go and no reason to get there if there was.

When Phil and I got to the train station, there were the same old men sitting on the folding chairs. Well, they weren't really old; only one looked past sixty. The rest were in the prime of their lives. One man stood at the end of the platform near the parking lot, videotaping the arrival of a freight train. He had a beard and hair to his shoulders. All heads turned toward the train, turned with its passing, and watched as it disappeared around the curve. Then everything was quiet.

Phil unloaded my bags and I paid him. It was late afternoon, a clear, not-too-hot July day. "I'd stay here and make sure you were all right, if it was dark," he said. "The people here . . . you never know."

Just me and the train-watchers. "Looks pretty safe." I told

Phil thanks and tipped him big and settled in on the bench. As I waited, a pair of twenty-ish-or-so artistic-type guys put their bags down near mine—one kid, with a shaved head, had a Marlboro-labeled carry-on held together with duct tape; the other was trimmed up, with glasses and a backpack. Then a woman with a toddler and a man with two boys appeared, and we began our long wait. There was something seductive in anticipating freight line or Amtrak, in watching the cars pass by, each one different, carrying its own load. The platform quickly got familiar. The man with the white hair opened a room in the roped-off building. A cramped shabby office, it held a battered desk, file cabinets, and a Coke machine. Old train magazines were piled on the windowsill. A pot of weak coffee and a container of creamer rested on a table covered with Juicy Fruit and LifeSavers, crocheted doilies and heart-shaped magnets. A bench along one wall was littered with out-of-date newspapers, and there was just enough room to walk single-file through the debris. Have you ever been in grandparents' houses that hold themselves in times long past? This office was early '50s. That was when things were bought, and that was where the attitude remained. No television. No computer, cordless phone, or microwave. Just a transistor radio tuned to a baseball game.

I bought a fifty-cent Mountain Dew from the machine and went back to the platform. The train was already an hour past due, and the train-watchers conjectured a two-hour delay. ("'Course, that was when I called them back at their last stop. Who knows but that they've just been sitting on the tracks since.") I settled in on my bench and flipped open my *Outside* magazine. A jock in full gear was climbing the Himalayas. Another thrill-seeking journalist was bargaining with the Khmer Rouge. In Hooterville, the man with the two boys and the woman with the toddler sat together on the sidewalk near the tracks. The kids balanced the ties and tossed pebbles. My cousins and I used to challenge each other not to slip from steel to slats as we savored the dusty hot metal smell that is specifically train. "Come back," said the mother to the girl. The child giggled and ran to the rail beyond.

That was when Davy Jones of the Monkees walked by—or who we all decided was Davy Jones. He looked me right in the eye and I didn't recognize him, even though I had loved the Monkees as a kid, still owned and played their records (although I would've been a lot more worked up to see Micky or Mike). His shirt was half unbuttoned, like he thought he looked good, but he showed his wear like blue jeans faded to white. I thought maybe he was a local thief, crazy even, someone who had some intelligence but ended, due to self-destruction or bad luck, drifting around railroad stations. When he went by again, I didn't look up.

I wasn't curious until the student-guys sauntered back down the platform. They were singing *Hey, hey, we're the Monkees,* and "(I'm Not Your) Stepping Stone," which impressed me, because how many twenty-year-olds know "(I'm Not Your) Stepping Stone"? "Davy Jones," one snickered. "Yeah, what's Davy Jones doing slinking around a train station in a ratty shirt and driving a fuckin' LTD, man." Actually, I could see it: with the prime of his career in 1968 and the Monkees reunions dismal failures highlighted by being blackballed by MTV for missing a performance date on a New Year's Eve special—after a life of forced cuteness and failed tours—sure, I could see Davy Jones driving a clunker. Even on TV he looked like an aging child, forced to be lovable and British after it was really too late.

The boys' voices grew sillier as their excitement increased, until finally the kid with the shaved head abruptly walked across the platform to the parking lot. There he struck up a conversation with the maybe-Davy, who smoked a cigarette as he leaned against a car. I recognized the shag haircut and fey stance and the profile and the crow's feet and suddenly he didn't look like a track derelict anymore, but someone seasoned, assured. The energy of the kid's adulation turned on a light, and there it was, that annoying bubbly cocky attitude of that wacky and fun-loving teenaged idol Davy had once been.

"Oh, man," said the kid who'd been left behind. "I don't believe it."

They both ended up hanging out with Davy Jones, or the person who was doing a great job of impersonating Davy Jones. I sauntered down the platform, pretending interest in the tracks. I thought about going over, but decided to preserve my ten-year-old Monkees mentality, when I believed that the world on TV was the real world that would exist if only I wasn't stuck in the middle of Nowhere, Illinois. In my TV memory, Davy continued his amusing antics with his three talented roommates, and somewhere in space they were causing loads of wacky trouble accompanied by a pop soundtrack of King/Goffin and Neil Diamond songs. I didn't want to believe that Davy had been relegated to rural Pennsylvania. Though maybe the maybe-Davy had made this choice. In a city, a former star would go unnoticed in favor of brighter, better-dressed lights; but here in Lewistown, Davy could remain that happy-go-lucky madcap who played Oliver before landing the job on *The Monkees*. While *The Monkees* made its four performers briefly famous, the show ended their careers. Though most critics admit that the Monkees were a pretty decent rock band, the group was fabricated for the TV show. The band was fake, but it was real, too. One rock scholar (yeah, they exist) conjectured that if Mike Nesmith hadn't joined the Monkees, making himself unserious to anyone over fifteen, he would have been the true leader of the alternative country music movement. His post-Monkees albums show this potential, but Nesmith could never get past the chimp stigma. (Trivia/literary reference: Mike Nesmith's mother invented Wite-Out. He has grown rich from writers' mistakes.) By allowing themselves to be Hooterized, made perfect and perfectly silly, the guys in the Monkees became a joke. I did not want to see a Davy who looked like he might be coming off of a three-day speed run. I wanted to see him twenty-one, singing "Valleri" and tapping a tambourine on a day-glo flower-power stage.

When the boys got back, I couldn't help it—I asked them what it was like. "Got his autograph, man." The one with the shaved head and tattoos got all goofy, a big macho tattooed boy. "He lives here, raises race horses, owns a studio, is waiting for his manager. I got his address and phone number, man, and he might even record us." He hugged his friend. "Wild shit always happens when we get together, I shoulda known." His friend just smiled.

Later, in the café car, the shaved-head kid told everyone who'd listen about how he met Davy Jones in the middle of freaking nowhere. The café car, filled with smoke and beer drinkers of every size, age, and color, listened to his story. In Lewistown, nobodies became somebody.

I finally realized my childhood dream of seeing a Monkee. The possible Davy Jones had gotten back into his LTD, but not before catching my eye with that thrill of recognition—the thrill of knowing that *I* recognized *him*—making him look, from a distance, like that wacky fake-Beatle who'd been the poster-boy heartthrob of every ten-year-old girl in Illinois. Before I stepped up into the train, the white-haired man in the lawn chair waved goodbye. Just like Uncle Joe at the end of the show. "Y'all come back now, hear," I expected him to say. Maybe I just missed the episodes that had the neighbor dying of black lung and Eb beating his wife and Mr. Green Jeans selling the farm; the three lovely sisters growing old and slipping into boring backwoods marriages. I guess we always knew they were there; like real life, we just didn't want to see them.

getting out to new places

GRADUATION

BALLOONS HANG FROM my cousin's mailbox, a cluster of school colors—a burst of unity pride, the last time blue and orange will matter in quite this way to the graduate. Cassie and I went to Rochester High, just like my mother and aunt. My class, by the time everyone had dropped out from pregnancies and boredom, had fifty-eight kids. My mom's had nineteen. Cassie's has more than one hundred-fifty. Rochester grew from its borders like a chrysanthemum, gathering stragglers. Consolidation conquered the tiniest schools, throwing one community into another. Five basketball teams merged into one; five small towns lost their identities, their gathering spots. The school Cassie's father went to is closed.

"Orange and blue's the colors; Rockets is the name; Spirit is the reason; We're going to win this game." I felt trapped, labeled, and bored in Rochester, where I was from fifth grade on. I blamed the school, figuring it would be different "out there" in the big world—but, of course, there really isn't an "out there." To fit means to give up something of self, to compromise and trade off, and I couldn't do it. No one in my family ever lets go. Our dominant spirit is obstinacy. It loses us as much, at least, as it wins us. But we keep going—sarcastic survivors of war, early marriage, dead children, insanity, illness. My cousin's daughters, and mine, seem to have inherited this tenacity, which reassures me in terms of our survival. We pass down our stubbornness as surely as we did the wheat-patterned plates found free in boxes of early '60s detergent—'cause we know it'll be worth something someday.

My daughter Paige and I turn down Cousin Mike's gravel drive, psyching up for the graduation party. We park behind a string of Ford pick-ups and Oldsmobiles, get out of the Toyota and head hesitantly up the steps and into the house. This is only the third time I've been to Mike's; since I'm the city cousin, all of sixty miles away, I don't have time or reason to visit. Family gatherings nearly always take place at our parents' houses, and once that generation dies, I don't know. Maybe I won't see my cousins anymore.

"I like the country kids," Paige had said in the car, as we drove down an Illinois back road, "but I'm not sure they know what to do with me. Sometimes they say things and I don't know what they're saying!"

"Like what?"

"Like . . . I don't know. They talk funny. And they play games funny. But they think I play games funny. So it's weird. But I like them." She looked back at her murder mystery while the CD player boomed out "Rhapsody in Blue."

Mike lives in a house of his own construction and design across from my aunt and uncle's old home in Roby. He doesn't live right on the river, but it would take him five minutes to walk back there. Mike and his wife, Bonnye, raised four daughters— the first, Cassandra, the graduate, born when Mike was only seventeen. The girls all have C-names: Cassie, Charissa, Caitlin, and Calla. Another daughter, only two, died in her crib; her C-name was Courtney. This baby was born just a month before my daughter and was buried on a freezing day in an isolated hill cemetery. My mother told me it was an aneurysm, a remnant of a traumatic birth. Mike blames an antibiotic that the baby took for a cold. The documents called it SIDS. Mike and Bonnye had no insurance.

A long time passed before Mike was the same. Bonnye, a placid and resigned farm daughter, never lost her look of ancient watchfulness. When Cassie was old enough to take care of her sisters, Bonnye got a job at J.C. Penney's working layaway. Penney's was the Springfield store nearest the highway that took Bonnye home. The stress of work, chores, and raising four daughters wore her out before she was thirty. In high school, she was an inspired musician with a natural ear and no formal training. She taught her oldest how to play trumpet and this won Cassie a scholarship to The Juilliard School of Music.

"She turned it down," my cousin Brenda tells me, as we hang out in Mike's converted basement. When we first came in, Paige and I had said brief hellos, grabbed food (the usual turkey, mashed potatoes, corn, and jello salad), and headed downstairs. That's where I found most of my family. Brenda's tone is disinterested; she doesn't know or care much about Juilliard. My mom had referred to the scholarship, when I talked to her on the phone, as "some music school out East"—implied shrug. "Mike decided it was too far," says Brenda. "Plus she'd have to travel all over the country on tour. Think of all the trouble she'd get into." Brenda, my shrinking buttercup cousin, had grown into a large, muscular woman with big hair and an attitude. Struggles with Uncle Wade over things like the right to wear jeans instead of dresses so embittered her that she has the freedom of meanness. After six months in a Springfield apartment, she married Ron, a construction worker like her dad. She was barely eighteen. Ron's one of those affable, low-key guys who is liked by all and tolerates life with deadpan good humor. While Brenda rattles on about Juilliard, Ron opens the door and looks out at the yard.

"It was her band leader got her to apply. He thought she was real good. It's kind of hard to see the point." Brenda's daughter, Kierstin, perches on the arm of the flowered sofa, and Brenda runs her hands through the girl's hair. She raises the mane, lets it drop, watches it fan. All of my cousins' girls have hair to their waists. "I mean, the trumpet. You can't really *do* anything, playing the trumpet. It's not like there's a job in it. It's more a hobby."

The irony of saying this to a writer is lost on her. I think it is, anyway. "She could teach," I suggest.

"You have to move away to get those jobs."

I can't argue. The option—that moving might be all right—isn't in the room. To introduce it would cause everyone to move out the door, confirmed in their belief that I'm still a danger. I lived in New York. I lived in Los Angeles. I live in Bloomington, Illinois, in a city of a hundred-thousand, which to them would be confining and too upwardly-mobile-white-collar—and I teach college, beyond the imagination of people who have never set foot on a campus. I'm pretty sure they think I plan riots and implant radical ideas into the brains of impressionable small-town kids. (Which isn't really far from wrong. . . .)

"So what's she doing?" I ask, not sure I want to know, feeling an old sneaking blues brought by lost opportunities, mine and theirs. I don't want to tip them off. I don't want to judge, or admit to judging. There's no turning my cousins from their views. College is an oblique and risky world to them. Look at me. Divorced, remarried, and moved away. If they granted that my life worked out, it would make them feel small. I don't want to make them feel like that. I know that my decisions were right, were inevitable, for me, but I feel no arrogance. There are so many decisions I would like to rewind and replay. I just needed to write.

Brenda looks to my mom, who stands across the room with Grandma. They claim to be more comfortable standing; if they sit on the overstuffed couch, they say, they won't be able to get back up. Keeping the ends open for escape is what they're doing. I sit on the arm of the couch, and between Brenda and me is Heather, my youngest cousin's wife, who never says a word except to the toddler who hunches on the floor between her knees.

"Eastern," Mom says, meaning Eastern Illinois University, a state school about fifty miles south, in the middle of nowhere. "She wants to take marine biology."

"But why?" I blurt.

"She has friends there, I guess," says Mom, meeting my eye in a significant way. She knows how I will feel about this.

I look at the floor, at the toddler messing with some Pokémon figure. Juilliard for Eastern. Music for biology. She has to go to Juilliard! I want to sing, schemes running through my head. But at Christmas I tried to get Cassie to audition at

Millikin, where I teach, which at least has a fine music program. She never did. If she won't go to Decatur because it's too dangerous, she surely won't go to New York City.

I feel sad about my gentle second cousin with the wavy hair, the one who took care of the children, who was at all times gracious. I've never heard her play the trumpet. Her ability is as taken for granted and accepted as Mike's lovely garden and Joe's upgrade to detective and Charissa's quick jokes. To them, a talent is the same as anything else requiring care and nurturance. And they're right. But it's *Juilliard,* a school I walked past with high envy when I lived in New York, admiring the musicians who bustled to the subway carrying cellos and flutes. But who am I to say? I blew off just about every get-ahead chance I had so I could stay in Illinois. My shot at New York ambition went as belly-up as a captured fish when I couldn't adapt to the ozone levels and the garbage and the drive-bys (the Korean gangs were at war on the street ten flights down) and the beggars who squatted in the ATMs. I couldn't adjust to graffiti and angry stares. Even though I lived on Broadway, with its big names and famous delis, its energy flew past me like the subway in the hole. My New York wasn't a Woody Allen world. So say Cassie went to Juilliard. She might've given up. Maybe it's better not to know. To keep a dream, to be consoled by "what if?" I used to think "what if?" would be the worst question, implying a lack of daring. Now I wonder if it's better to avoid the answer.

"Eastern's okay," I say. Amazing she's going to college at all. The first one, other than me. And a girl, at that.

"Music's a good hobby," says Brenda.

My arguments would hold no weight. I've been throwing them out to my family since I was six, and there is no fighting their certainty that there is value in home, that physical work is what counts, that thought and art are silly decoration, some elaborate pretense—bullshit and lies. They know what I think, anyway. I know what they think, anyway.

Cassie, subject of this talk, is upstairs hosting her party. When Paige and I first came in, Bonnye, her mom, hovered near the living room piano, as if it consoled her; Mike stood in a corner of the kitchen, chatting with an in-law. I asked him how he was doing. "Hiding," he said. He didn't introduce me to the in-law. Nobody introduced anybody. We aren't good at that sort of thing.

Bonnye's family stayed on one side of the living room. Farmers, they were a step above the Pattons, and dressed in their best. Far too reticent to enter into that lake of stolidity, I didn't cross the room to observe the skylight Mike had installed in his high-beamed ceiling, a feature that refracted afternoon light upon the faces of the good citizens. Nearly all of the Pattons and Becks—our side of the family—only ventured up from the basement when they were hungry. After awhile, Mike came down, too.

As an adult, he looks much as he did when he was a kid—stocky, strong, thoughtful—except for a well-tended beard for that mountain-man image. He shows off the computer cabinet he built, which hides the machinery behind doors and has intricate CD slots. Then he talks about the wood stove and what work he still needs to do on it. A project is never finished, because nothing we do is perfect. Children walk in and out, girls full of smart-mouth and spirit. Charissa, I heard, has snuck smokes since the age of fourteen and has driven her car into fields three times on party nights—three times that we know of. A math and science whiz, she's already, at sixteen, been offered scholarships. She decided on Southern, a state school an hour away, without even applying to University of Chicago, MIT, or other places that might open their wallets to a working-class, female, science/math brain.

"Why should I let you have the car?" Mike challenges. Charissa stands with one hand on a pushed out hip, the other held out for bounty.

"Come on, Dad. It's not like there's anything I can really *do*."

"You'll find something."

The three teenage girls, Charissa and her friends, dissolve in giggles. "No, we won't, Dad."

After a couple of stories about the dangers of drunk driving, of not going anyplace other than where you're supposed to, he lets her go.

"Man!" one of the girls says, as they dart up the stairs. "Your dad is *tough*!"

Mike meets my eye, shaking his head in that beaten-down way of parents resolved to fate. He's only thirty-five, and already his oldest is leaving home. At Cassie's birth, he was forced to work in his father's business; his path was sealed. Before the kids, he talked of being an architect—he'd been drawing his own painstakingly detailed designs since he was twelve. What he wants to be now is an organic gardener, to own his own farm and greenhouse and sell vegetables and flowers. He's good at this, too. But instead, he has become Patton Construction, an eldest son inheriting his father's legacy.

"Want to look at the yard?" he asks shyly. A rainy day turned hesitant sun. His property stretches to the blacktop county road on one side and then in all directions, ending at timber that lines the back road into Roby—the same road we walked as kids. The only visible houses are far in the distance; only the traffic on the county road reminds us of scattered neighbors. What's striking about the land isn't its size, but its maintenance. Flowers, vines, bushes, and trees placed in proximity and distance so that one plant highlights another. Forget weeds. Forget randomness. Unlike my so-called garden, where daisies loom over small delicate flowers with forgotten names, and sun-loving plants struggle to hold their own in half-shade, and groundcover is nothing more than an excuse not to mow, Mike's vegetation actually *goes* together. The shape and texture of leaves and blossoms are taken into account. Purpose and design considered when placing trees for windbreak. The garden is where Mike belongs.

As we walk—me and Mom and Grandma—he relays the names of the plants in the nearest beds. "Spiderwort," Mike fingers a sharp-petaled blue flower, "was used in the old days to get rid of a spider bite. And this here is St. John's Wort—the same stuff in the drugstore. You can plant these yourself, you know. Then you don't need anything else. I got my vegetables back there—" He points to a hefty plot near the fence row. "Tomatoes and carrots and peas and corn and what-all. And I got a grape arbor over there—" He waves to where vines twine. Turning to his favorites, he displays the flowers and bushes—the show-pieces planted around the side of the house, along the driveway, to the front. His home has an old-fashioned porch of a kind seen less and less in Illinois, but still prevalent in Kentucky and Tennessee: a "sittin' porch" with carved, clematis-covered white rails. It looks out upon a yard that goes on, dotted with circular beds.

Must be hard as hell to mow, I think, and Mike apparently reads my mind because he says, "My girls have a hell of a time mowing this thing. You can tell there because of how that grass is getting up along the sides. I meant to clip it back before the party. . . . Ever since Katie smacked into this tree here, she's been a little cautious." He laughs, ducking his head.

Since the girls aren't in a zillion competitions, the way suburban kids are, they work around the land, just as we did as children. Their knowledge and experience of the world around them goes deep, rather than wide.

I wonder if the girls resent it. If they dream themselves into cities of shops and clubs. If they want to join gymnastics and dance and volleyball teams. If they want designer clothes and video games that their parents can't and won't buy. Do they feel deprived, less able to make their way through the complications of a wired society? Or do they accept the mowing, planting, cleaning, caretaking on land that, in all directions, is theirs?

"How do you keep up?" My own small flower patch is more than I can handle; the idea of my daughter maneuvering a riding mower is just funny. I can teach students and write stories, and Paige can draw elaborate cartoons and play the saxophone, but all this physical outdoor work would just be too big.

"I come out here every evening, when I can." He'd be out there all day, if he could, rather than hauling two-by-fours and pounding nails. Construction is dangerous labor, hard on the body even without accidents. My youngest cousin, Kirk, worked construction with Mike and Uncle Wade until he fell off a roof. Back operations and a metal rod later, he is in continuous pain, moving like a scarecrow. Now Kirk works in a tile store while his wife baby-sits. They're raising two kids on their own spot of land. The family, all of them, is always a step away from losing it all, yet they get by. A parent helps a child, a sibling a sibling, a child a parent. As the girls go to college, will they want or even be able to take care of Mike and Bonnye, or take on property? A profession away from the land probably means they can no longer live on it; careers swallow so much time and energy. Our jobs dictate our identities and demand we move away, and we do it. We like this freedom. It's easier to go from point to point than to stay and dig a laborious hole. When the girls go to college, they may learn to look down on their background or to idealize it in the glow of nostalgia, or hide it in defense, or all of these. In the kitchen, talking about going to Cassie's college orientation, Mike had said, "She'll probably end up knowing her old man is stupid." Seems inevitable. At school, we work hard to gain this new wider perspective. But we forget that depth strikes gems and oil and bedrock, that ties matter, even if they don't get us a higher salary or a notch of respectability. It's easier that way. When we forget, we don't have to face what we left behind.

Standing in Mike's yard, facing Buckhart Creek—that tributary of the Sangamon which is a tributary of the Illinois which is a tributary of the Mississippi—I count the number of lives I've walked through. People who I knew well and moved away from, like closing a book. People who I barely knew, or knew in the way of surface jobs and "contacts," brushing and leaving. I've done it so often I'm good at it, even philosophical. Hurt and disappointment may write the ending—or maybe rejection, or failure, or advancement, or necessity, or restlessness. Or the ending is written for me and I have no power to change it. I wander from group to group, house to house, job to job, place to place. I have lived in more than twenty houses since I was eighteen and I know I'm not in my final home. I hate the uncertainty, yet I wouldn't like to be like Mom—a life in a monotonous, draining job—or Mike, stuck in the routine of pounding nails, injuring his back, his arms, his legs. My uncle, who's done it all his life, moves in slow-motion, he's so crippled by the physical stress of hauling, lifting, balancing. Though I live elsewhere, I still see Mike's land, and my mother's, and all of Christian and Sangamon Counties as my point of reference, pivot, jump. Many don't have this much of a home. The mall and the subdivision and the chain restaurant are their places—familiar spots that reassure us that wherever we go, it will be the same. My family and I are so out of step. We don't even like malls.

"I didn't realize Cassie was going," Mike says, "until that orientation at the school. I didn't think much of it, to be honest." He shrinks when he remembers this. I see that a lot with country people when they go into the urban world. I see it in myself. The way my husband's parents slink down in their seats when they go to a play at my stepkids' upscale high school. The way Mom has never set foot on a college campus, not even for my graduation. Sometimes I barely believe that I teach at one every day. We learn not to understand one another. One person looks pretentious; another, illiterate. In our new smart world, we categorize and label. The people we grew up with become "working class," or "struggling farmers," or "the last agrarians"—or, getting down to it, "white trash," "hicks," "bohunks." Here's a joke I heard in

getting out to new places

grad school: *Q: What do you call a Marxist from the Ozarks? A: A redneck.* We can't go back. But we can never entirely get away.

"I wish I had all of this land," I say. But I haven't earned it and Mike knows that. While I've been out having bright conversations, he's been working and saving and gardening. You wouldn't know what to do with it, is the look he gives me. I'd be like the city folks who come out to live off the land, only to hire someone else to take care of the yard. Mike knows, because he builds their houses.

As Mom and Grandma and I head toward our cars, Cassie, the graduate, comes out to say goodbye. She is tall and self-possessed in an unassuming way. Her blond hair over time has taken on brown, leaving it a honey-color, and her placid face is dotted with freckles. She's gotten past her family's embarrassment at social events; she's learned, probably at school, how to politely say hello, to shake a hand or offer a hug, and to politely say goodbye.

"Thank you for coming," she smiles.

I want to take her by the shoulders (even though she's a lot taller). *Are you sure? Have you thought this through? Can you really give up a chance like this? This is Juilliard, Cassandra!* Maybe she'll get to college and the independence gene will kick in. Maybe she'll see that the vision overrides the momentary job and will take the trumpet in hand. I wonder if she has a secret dream. If, like most artists, she imagines playing Carnegie Hall, or cutting a jazz album, or being reviewed in the *New York Times*. The poet in me wants her to push to the farthest edge, to go deep into talent through work, the way her father cares for his garden. If she has to be selfish, break ties, hurt people, then do it. Yet another part of me—seeing her gentleness and calm and the way the breeze lifts the hem of her Penney's dress, seeing the way she sizes up her world like leveling a board, centering the bubble—wonders if she'll have a better life near the Sangamon, with children maybe and animals, playing whatever music she wants, playing for herself. Or is that my dream?

GRADUATION

notes

p. 98   Quotes from interviews are from articles published in the *State Journal-Register,* Springfield, Illinois.

p. 101   John Mellencamp, "Pink Houses." *Uh-Huh.* Mercury Records, 1983.

p. 130   Curtis W. Ellison, *Country Music Culture: From Hard Times to Heaven* (Jackson: University Press of Mississippi, 1995).

p. 133   Nicholas Dawidoff, *In the Country of Country* (New York: Vintage Books, 1998).

pp. 137–138   Bill DeMain, "The Roots of an American Songwriter: John Mellencamp." *Performing Songwriter* 4, no. 23 (March/April 1997).

p. 139   Bob Guccione, Jr., "Fanfare for the Common Man: Who Is John Mellencamp?" *Spin,* February 1992.

p. 145   John Mellencamp, "Eden Is Burning." *John Mellencamp.* Columbia Records, 1998.

p. 146   Christopher Scapelliti, "Rebel Without a Cure." *Guitar World Acoustic* no. 28 (November 1998).

BECKY BRADWAY

is a writer whose creative-nonfiction essays and short stories have appeared in *DoubleTake, North American Review,* and *American Fiction,* among other publications. She lives in Normal, Illinois, with her husband, three children, and assorted pets. After working as an editor, secretary, janitor, Dairy Queen server, and UPS clerk—to name just a few of her former occupations—she now teaches creative writing and U.S. Studies at Millikin University in Decatur, Illinois.

RAYMOND BIAL

has published more than fifty critically acclaimed books of black-and-white and color photographs for children and adults. These include a series of books on Native American tribes; other titles of interest include, most recently, *A Handful of Dirt, The Ghost of Honeymoon Creek, Ghost Towns of the American West,* and *One-Room School.* A full-time librarian, he lives with his wife and three children in Urbana, Illinois.

KATHARINE WRIGHT

has had photographs published in newspapers and as post-cards, and her poetry has appeared in several journals. She has taught creative writing, ESL, and children's literature at several universities and has worked as a zookeeper in upstate New York. Her current projects include a year-long photographic study of children at play and a words-and-pictures memoir having to do with her zoo experiences. She lives in State College, Pennsylvania, with her husband and daughter.

BOOK AND JACKET DESIGNER sharon sklar

COPYEDITOR kendra boileau stokes

COMPOSITOR sharon sklar

TYPEFACES minion and frutiger

BOOK AND JACKET PRINTER thomson-shore